Pastoral Counseling

Pastoral Counseling
THE BASICS

James E. Dittes

Westminster John Knox Press
Louisville, Kentucky

For information, address Westminster John Knox Press, 100 Witherspoon Street, Louisville, Kentucky 40202-1396.

Scripture quotations, unless otherwise noted, are from the New Revised Standard Version of the Bible, copyright © 1989 by the Division of Christian Education of the National Council of the Churches of Christ in the U.S.A., and are used by permission.

Book design by Sharon Adams
Cover design by Brooke Griffiths

First edition

Published by Westminster John Knox Press
Louisville, Kentucky

This book is printed on acid-free paper that meets the American National Standards Institute Z39.48 standard. ♾

PRINTED IN THE UNITED STATES OF AMERICA
99 00 01 02 03 04 05 06 07 08 — 10 9 8 7 6 5 4 3 2 1

Library of Congress Cataloging-in-Publication Data

Dittes, James E.
    Pastoral couseling / by James E. Dittes. — 1st ed.
        p.   cm.
    ISBN 0-664-25738-0 (alk. paper)
    1. Pastoral counseling. I. Title.
BV4012.2.D565   1999
253.5—dc21   98-33352

For Anne,
extraordinary witness

Contents

Preface

This book records what I have learned in forty-five years of teaching pastoral counseling at Yale Divinity School. It is not so much that I have found my questions about pastoral counseling answered; rather, it is that the questions have changed.

The slightly panicky questions of the beginning counselor are still there: How can I respond? How can I say the right thing? How can I help? How can I make a difference? How can I bridge the differences in social background between the counselee and myself? How can I stay psychologically adept and theologically faithful at the same time? Psychologically sensitive and ethically responsible? ("Ethically" refers not just to the daunting dilemmas of personal conduct that emerge in counseling conversations but also to the still more daunting dilemmas of social injustice that shape and misshape the lives we want to rescue.) How do I help the helpless in ways that don't abet the helplessness, but empower? How do I counsel the same people I have to preach to and the same people I have to ask for a satisfactory housing allowance?

All the perplexing "how" questions persist.

But they dissolve, too, into more fundamental questions: "what" questions. Just what *is* pastoral counseling? What am I doing when I do pastoral counseling? What is happening to the counselee, to me, between us? (For the sake of clarity about the fundamentals, the discussion here is limited to the exchange between two people.) In what ways is my life being joined to and intervening in the life of another? What is pastoral about pastoral counseling? What makes pastoral counseling different from other pastoring, if it is? What is the connection between pastoral counseling and the church community? Is pastoral counseling part of God's call to ministry? Or is it a self-satisfying and desperate attempt to flee or to salvage a faltering ministry by imitating the more prestigious "mental health" professionals? In pastoral counseling, am I advancing or obstructing God's intentions for God's people?

So the "what" questions dissolve into the still more fundamental "who" questions: Who am I when I am pastoral counselor? Or perhaps, more urgently, *whose* am I? On whose behalf am I acquiring the role of pastoral counselor? What persona am I taking on when I respond to that ordaining call, "Do you have time to talk with me?" What commitments, promises—even what vows, what renunciations—am I making? What boundaries, what self-definitions, what goals am I setting? What role, what niche in others' lives, am I stepping into? What roles and expectations am I declining to fill? "Who do they say that I am?"

Notice, too, that "why" questions are evoked—more ultimate questions like "Why do pastoral counseling?" and more immediate questions like "Why make a particular response to a particular counselee at a particular moment?" This book does not aspire to tell you what to say to a counselee—how to fill in the pauses, for example, in the two conversations that are recorded on the next pages, at the beginning of the Introduction. But this book does want to help you know *why* you say what you do, and for that we turn to the "what" and "who" questions.

Just as a pastoral counseling conversation may peel away urgent and immediate questions in order to identify and explore still more urgent and fundamental questions, so this book tries to look through the pressing "how" questions to consider the more fundamental questions that will ultimately provide answers to the "how" questions.

So if this book tries to depict and deploy the *fundamentals* of pastoral counseling, it is therefore also *introductory*. It is "introductory" not just in the obvious curricular or hierarchical sense of that word. This is a first pass at the issues, and much more needs to be said—although that is quite true. There is indeed much more to be said about pastoral counseling than appears in these pages, especially how these fundamentals are expressed and applied in varying settings and situations and by counselors of varying personal styles. However, I wouldn't want the fundamentals to be lost in the course of that elaboration.

This book aspires to be "introductory" in the stronger social or relational sense of the word. ("Noncounselor, please meet pastoral counseling.") I want to introduce pastoral counseling to those not familiar or comfortable with it in a way that may encourage some familiarity and comfort. I think the focus on the basics can help that to happen.

It is the "how" questions that convey the inevitable anxieties of the counselor. They often seem to imply a demand for expertise and skill, for training and experience, which few pastoral counselors ever achieve. How can I know the right thing to say? How can I make the right diagnosis? How can I deliver whole-hearted unconditional love? How can I be a good counselor? Even a good-enough counselor? "I can't" is the honest answer. The focus on the fundamentals, on the "what" and "who" questions, may take the pressure off by taking the focus off the pastoral counselor's knowings and doings. This book does not promise to help a pastor meet high "professional" criteria and to win credentials or "success." Indeed the book challenges the tyranny of the expectation that pastoral counseling is identified by a mastery of information or technical proficiency or successful cases. It suggests that pastoral counseling is, finally, more a matter of the heart or the soul than the head, more a matter of faith than works, an attitude and posture more than a technique or skill. What makes one a pastoral counselor is something more like a personal conversion than a medical residency, more like a religious commitment than a licensing syllabus. The postures of pastoral counseling are available to all. If they are difficult or strenuous, it is not an intellectual strain but an existential strenuousness that must always accompany a call to trust, that is, a call to surrender just those preoccupations with "selfhood" or ego that are ensconced in concern about technique and credentials.

If focus on fundamentals eases concerns about how demanding and formidable pastoral counseling is, it also may address the common apprehension that pastoral counseling is subversive. To some, pastoral counseling seems to value, permissively, the individual's needs and preferences in a way that severely contradicts a minister's commitment to building a community and to fostering responsible citizenship in the world and the kingdom. I share commitment to community and citizenship. Pastoral counseling is offered here as a *means* towards such maturity of person and faith, not as a *model* for maturity of person and faith. The strategies and attitudes of pastoral counseling arrayed in this book are not offered as end products of ministry but as one process of ministry. The role of the counselee no more defines the Christian life than the role of counselor defines Christian ministry. Far from celebrating the status quo or the private realm, pastoral counseling joins other dimensions of ministry in the call to re-call, re-deem, re-vision life into being less like it has been and more as it is intended.

Introduction

Here are two typical conversations that call a minister to pastoral counseling. We report only the counselee's remarks and the pauses. The purpose of this book is to discover how the pastoral counselor responds during those pauses.

ALICE

Alice, about 45, fairly active in the church where you minister, has called you to apologize for missing the "Cleanup Day" last Saturday and to ask if she can meet with you to discuss what work still needs to be done. She arrives at your office at the appointed time. Here is her part of the conversation. She pauses now and then, waiting for you to respond.

> I'm really sorry about disappearing last Saturday. I want to make it up. You must have thought I was sleeping in. I only wish I had been.

> I got this weird letter from Dad last Friday that just didn't make any sense, and when I tried to call him that night, he made less sense. So I had to run up there Saturday to see what was going on.

Introduction

He's talking about ripping out all the shrubbery around his place and putting in sod. At least I think that's what he's talking about. He acts like I should know all about it, keeps saying I warned him about ticks. But I never heard of any of this.

I couldn't just skip it. You know how when he talked about swapping cars last fall, and I didn't follow up on it, how he screwed that up.

First thing he said when he saw me drive up last Saturday was, "Did you come on 63 or 117? You know it's three miles shorter on 117." I can never get him to realize that 117 goes through the center of two towns, with all that traffic. I should know—I've had to make that trip enough.

Well, which road would you take?

I never know when he's going to pull one of these things. Sol and I promised ourselves we would finally take our "honeymoon" to Spain next fall. But I don't dare leave the country now, what with him and Sol's mother's bad heart.

Yeah, I thought with both boys out of the house, we could lead our own lives. But it's like I have one more adolescent to worry about.

When will these battles ever end?

Why couldn't he just give me a hug when I got out of the car and say, "Glad to see you"?

These are the things Alice says to you. How do you respond?

MURRAY

Suppose that, at the end of the same day as the conversation with Alice, you are returning to your office after an evening meeting with church officers. Murray, about 45, active in the church, catches up with you at the door of your office and asks, "Do you have a minute?" You do have time and invite him to sit down. He starts talking, leaving pauses for you to respond.

> I was talking with Sam before the meeting and thought you ought to know what he is going through. Maybe you should talk with him, or maybe find him some volunteer work to do in the church office.

> Well, I think he is finding retirement hard. His heart is still in the office. He asked me tonight if the year-end inventory at the shop was going to go smoothly. You know, he was real proud of the inventory control system he set up. He would go in on Saturdays to keep it fine-tuned.

> Well, the whole truth is that now we just scan bar codes in and scan bar codes out, and the computer keeps track of everything that's on the shelves. We just scrapped Sam's system. But I can't remind him of that. It's still his baby.

> I don't think Sam was ready for retirement. He doesn't seem to have any hobbies or anything.

> I hope I don't make that same mistake. When I get there, I want to have something in my life besides the job.

> It's a good thing I've got a few years, because I sure don't have time for hobbies now, no time for anything these days. I've got to get home now and polish a prospectus the boss wants on his desk tomorrow morning. Sally's going to be upset when she hears that.

> You're lucky not to be in this rat race.

> I guess the truth is, I get high on work. Polishing that prospectus is like my hobby, making it say just what I want to say, then getting it formatted until it really looks good. Not good, perfect.

Introduction

And it makes me feel like I have my hands on the levers of power, making good stuff happen, and really making a difference.

But then I have to remember what happened to Sam—no inventory control system, and no life either.

As pastoral counselor, how do you respond? How do you fill in the pauses? Is your response as "pastoral counselor" different from other possible "pastoral" responses, different from other "counseling"? How can you tell if you should even regard these conversations as pastoral counseling? These are the questions this book intends to address.

This book does not write a script for you to follow. Though it does suggest, especially in chapters 5 and 6, some of the more likely pastoral counseling responses to Alice and Murray, there is really no one right way to fill in the blanks. The book is less concerned with determining *what* you should say during the pauses than it is with encouraging you to know *why* you say what you do. What are the fundamental principles of pastoral counseling that guide you as you choose and perceive what you want to say to Alice and Murray—and to all the other Alices and Murrays you encounter in your ministry without the luxury of taking the time we have available in these pages to ponder the choices? Fundamentally, it is a question of identity: who—and whose—are you when you are a pastoral counselor?

WHAT IS PASTORAL COUNSELING?

The conversations with Alice and Murray help us to begin to notice the point of view the book takes towards these questions: What is pastoral counseling? Who is the pastoral counselor?

Introduction

Pastoral Counseling Is Often Disguised

The conversations with Alice and Murray portray situations that are characteristically ambiguous. In these conversations, no one uses the words *pastoral counseling*. Though you probably think of the conversation as pastoral counseling, the counselees probably do not.

Most pastoral counseling comes by surprise and in disguise, not by appointment and clearly separated from non-counseling encounters. This is not the well-defined session in which someone says "I want pastoral counseling," makes an appointment, arrives at your office on time, works hard for fifty minutes as textbook counselees usually do, and then leaves, perhaps to see you again a week later, but not before. These are more typical encounters, in which you can never be sure, from beginning to end, whether this is pastoral counseling. But it's not the time for debating definitions or negotiating goals. All you can do is act as though this is pastoral counseling, in case it is.

"I Need to Talk about Me"

No one in these conversations with Alice and Murray uses the word *self* or *soul*. But that is the topic of these conversations, as it is always the topic of pastoral counseling. What will become of me? What have I done? What can I do? What must I do? How do I fit into God's Creation? In the kingdom? In the community? What value do I have? What values do I live by? Can you hear these questions reverberating in Alice's and Murray's comments? Expressed and coded in the language of events and emotions and concrete problems and particular human relationships, in daily comings and goings, it is the status of the self, the fate of the soul that propels pastoral counseling. Pastoral counseling is always triggered by a concrete precipitating or so-called presenting problem, a missed commitment to clean up a church, a sense of distress over a friend's career change. What makes a person a pastoral counselee is the readiness to deepen and broaden the discussion of that precipitating problem to an exploration of more general and fundamental questions about his or her life. In these conversations, Alice and Murray do open up to themselves.

Many people assume that pastoral counseling refers to any conversation a pastor and parishioner may have about any one of a relatively limited roster of "pastoral" issues, such as death, illness, faith, family relations, alcoholism, or sexual indiscretion or other damaging behavior patterns. But many conversations on these topics may lack the attitudes of soul-searching that characterize pastoral counseling. And, as Alice and Murray illustrate, any dilemma or event in life, not just conventional "pastoral" issues, can occasion pastoral counseling.

A person's readiness to be a pastoral counselee is never clearly communicated because the readiness is never clear. Are Alice and Murray calling you to pastoral counseling? Are they saying, in so many words, "Something about me is troubling me" or "I want to talk about me and how I fit my life"? Or is Alice simply saying, "I want to talk about the church cleanup"? Is the discussion about her father a distraction from her main topic, or is it an unfolding pathway to her main topic? You cannot know. Probably she does not know. Whatever the case, you cannot surmise *what* may be troubling her, nor can you assume that she knows. This is not the time (if there is ever such a time) to speculate in diagnostic labels: Guilt? Compulsion? Alienation from church and faith? Ambivalence towards authority or responsibilities? Insomnia? This is not the time to explain to Alice the commitments you expect from a pastoral counselee. This is not the time to press Murray to talk about his own life instead of planning pastoral attention for Sam or to become vulnerable and express his own feelings.

But neither is this the time to rule out the possibility that Alice and Murray do, however ambiguously, however reluctantly, however indirectly, want to reflect, in some depth and some generality, on themselves and their own lives, that they want to be pastoral counselees. Your openness to hearing them in this way makes you a pastoral counselor.

More needs for pastoral counseling emerge out of chronic, slowly evolving feelings of alienation and distress than out of sudden crises like death and illness. Something about the events of last weekend—and you have no idea what, and don't need to—is one more instance of some larger pattern that is beginning to become painfully evident to Alice, however vaguely, indirectly, and allusively she may make her self-disclosure. Something about Sam's plight—perhaps you find out during the conversation what it is, and perhaps you don't—triggers some emerging quandary or distress for Murray. Pastoral counseling usually does not begin with neat, explicit, structured face-to-face fifty-minute conversations based on a clear contract and mutual expectations—the tidy way we would prefer.

If pastoral counseling, as ideally regarded, seems compromised by such ambiguity, the answer, I think, is to treat such less-than-ideal pastoral counseling with the same benign "as is" and "as if" trust with which, as we shall discover, pastoral counselors regard counselees and their less-than-ideal lives.

In the Mode of Confession

For pastoral counseling to occur, the counselee must be ready to be vulnerable, to discuss his or her life in the mode of confession, of surrender. Something is wrong, amiss, unfitting, not as it should be. I can't fix it by myself. I need help. I need to be different. I need a conversion.

This is an abrupt and frightening change from the common and well-practiced mode of functioning in the world, the mode of bravado and swagger, defensiveness and self-reliance. The counselee must be ready to abandon the conventional and comfortable selfhood as he or she has constructed it for the sake of rediscovering the self as created. This is hardly an easy and comfortable attitude for the counselee to adopt and maintain, and it is an important contribution of the counselor, as we shall see throughout the book, to provide the atmosphere that allows the candor of confession. But the counselee must be ready, or the counseling can't happen. Alice and Murray appear to be ready.

Pastoral Counseling Is Not Isolated

Pastoral counseling is usually precipitated out of an ongoing relationship between pastor and parishioner. This entangles the pastoral counseling in previous relationships between the two and in such ongoing concerns as cleanup day and Sam's welfare. This entanglement further complicates and compromises the distinctiveness of pastoral counseling. On the other hand, an existing relationship may facilitate pastoral counseling far more than it complicates it. It may provide the familiarity and trust that are prerequisite to pastoral counseling.

The ongoing pastoral relationship and church activities bring about counseling that would never otherwise happen. At face value, the cleanup day absence seems a small administrative problem easily solved and Alice's anxieties about it easily calmed. But there is also an urgency about her concern that calls for more earnest attentiveness. The chance to talk about the "administrative" problem makes possible the counseling-level attention. A minister's comings and goings afford unique access to people's lives. People's urgent concerns may be still masked in the routines of the comings and goings, but they are also revealed in these routines. A minister's day is full of privileged encounters in which a person's life is, momentarily and more or less, laid bare, confessed, and opened to healing, a day full of pastoral counseling. They are encounters in which a person almost dares to hope—just because you are a minister—for a touch of peace and well-being, a glimpse of wholeness and even holiness. What can seem to the minister a day full of casual or trivial exchanges, even nuisances and distractions, may be a day in which each exchange was the most important conversation that person had all day. Invited or not, ready or not, one after another, there is a blurted disclosure or plea, then a pause, a blank. How you respond can make a significant difference in how well your people live out their lives.

It is ironic that the very "administrative" work that the minister regards as impediment to pastoral work often becomes an occasion for pastoral counseling. It is more ironic that what the minister finds most annoying about administration—the irrational disproportion of energy and affect that people put into administrative issues (e.g., Alice's near-obsession with cleanup day)—is the reliable clue that pastoral counseling issues are lurking, that the episode carries a load of meaning, for the parishioner even though not for the minister.

The Pastor as Attentive Shepherd

When we consider the other half of the conversations with Alice and Murray, the counselor's half, what perspectives do we look for that characterize the event as pastoral counseling?

There are many ways to respond to Alice and Murray that are appropriate and helpful and pastoral. But not all of them would be deemed "pastoral counseling." The pastor may offer reassurance or advice on dealing with family or work problems. The pastor may remind Alice and Murray that others are going through similar dilemmas and may even put them in touch with others in the church community as a kind of ad hoc support group. The pastor may offer the resources of prayer and Bible study or church–press literature on midlife issues. The pastor may remind Alice and Murray of the resource of regular weekly worship. The pastor may raise the consciousness of Alice and Murray into understanding how their dilemmas are a kind of oppression from political and social forces or anomalies that should be contested and resisted.

These and others are all valid and potentially valuable pastoral responses. What mainly makes them different from pastoral counseling is that in these responses the pastor is setting an agenda, is defining the parishioner's problem, is delivering resources. Pastoral counseling is different. It is the pastoral response of providing the spiritual climate that maximizes the opportunity for the parishioner to grow in personhood and in the capacity to cope. The pastoral counselor empowers the *parishioner* to identify the problem and discover resources.

As pastoral counselor, your principal offering to Alice is a radically focused and attentive *witness* to her life, made possible by the radical renunciation of your role as a "player" in her life. As pastoral counselor, you are willing to lose yourself in the sense of being willing to totally disregard what any of the remarks or events mean to *you* in order to give your total attention to what they mean to *her*. For example, from your point of view as administrator, the work project may be finished, completed without Alice, and the cleanest response is to tell her this. But for the pastoral counselor, this is all irrelevant, set aside, and you focus on whatever it may mean to Alice to want to "make it up." For another example, Alice says, "You must have thought I was sleeping in." In a conventional social exchange, you may want to disclaim and correct her attribution ("No, I know what a hard worker you are."), or to parry it good-naturedly ("Well, I know I wished I were sleeping in."). But as pastoral counselor, you let yourself be unaffected by the attribution. You forget it, so you can attend totally to what the remark may mean to Alice.

We have said that the counselee brings to the pastoral counseling a readiness to abandon the self as constructed. Here, we say that this is matched—and fostered—by the counselor's readiness to abandon certain constructed dimensions of the counselor's own professional selfhood.

You disregard your own self-interest in favor of total regard for Alice. This makes it possible for her to do the same. For the brief occasional moments of pastoral counseling, she may taste the gracious freedom to disregard your reactions and preferences, to jettison all the anxious negotiations with which she has learned to maneuver her way through others' regard, and to bask in the experiment of regarding her own life unfiltered. This can't be unlike the experience of grace that derives from an awareness of a God who is willing to sacrifice self-interest for the sake of an unrelenting benign regard.

Introduction

Here, we take seriously the literal meaning of *pastor*, which is *shepherd*. *Pastoral* implies a special quality and intent of the relationship, a caring abundantly, a giving of self for the flock in one's charge. The pastor is totally and selflessly committed to the welfare of those under care, to their safety, to their growth, to their healing and holying (to spell the same word in both ways it has come to be spelled). The pastor is as self-abandoned as the prodigal father in offering embrace to the distressed and the lost (even though institutional obligations often bind the pastor to the maintenance role of the elder brother).

The pastoral counselor is self-conscious of being called and commissioned to this special, self-abandoned, caring relationship by a God who has made the commitment of self-abandoned caring the strategy of God's own ministry to the world. The pastor and the counseling he or she does is in response to a call by God to be an agent of God's purposes and hope for God's people.

What Is Pastoral Counseling?

The pastoral counseling conversation is like no other conversation. The pastoral counseling relationship is like no other, and perhaps is not even a relationship at all. It is unlike a conversation between friends or lovers, unlike a family conversation or a schoolroom conversation; it is even unlike most other pastoral conversations. Some things are missing, mainly an enmeshed mutuality. Some things are added, mainly an array of unfamiliar feelings. This difference is what makes it pastoral counseling and what makes it effective. But, like any other culture shock, it takes some getting used to, and it is difficult to sustain because it is difficult to trust. Both the counselee and the counselor find themselves wanting to revert to the familiar.

Introduction

If you are the counselee, you experience feelings you seldom experience in other conversations. You feel yourself safe, trusted, trusting, reprieved from expectations and sanctions, removed from the scramble and competition of the marketplace and transported into a momentary sanctuary. This is startling and hard to trust. It is not a relationship in which you can establish your place with the usual strategies and maneuvers. Honesty prevails. Honesty suffices.

Also, if you are the counselee, you feel, from somewhere inside yourself, unfamiliar hints of resentments, griefs, chagrin, doubt, and alienation and also unfamiliar hints of affection, faith, confidence, and self-assurance. This, too, is startling and hard to trust.

If you are the counselor, you experience your own kind of moratorium, even a transcendence, from involvement and mutuality. You are not looking for ways to bond, to play a role in this other person's life, or to fit the other into your life. Despite the intensity of the encounter, pastoral counseling is the opposite of an intimate mutuality. You do not care whether you like or are liked by the counselee. You do not need to carve out of this other's life a niche for yourself. You do not need to be manager, coach, healer, therapist, friend, or even pastor. You are immune from the need to make visible impact. Such conventional and habitual concerns are rendered irrelevant. You are called out of being a player in the other's life into becoming witness to it.

While the counselee's time-out from the scramble comes as a discovery and gift, yours comes as a deliberate vocational renunciation, the acceptance of the ascetic discipline of pastoral counseling. You experience a gracious nonchalance, a freely chosen willingness to let whatever will be, be—the template of the counselee's experience of sanctuary. "Let it be!" or "So be it!" becomes a profound affirmation of faith. But that is hard to trust because it so closely resembles the painful "let it be" or "so be it" of the subdued and hopeless. It is difficult to sustain the vocation of pastoral counseling. The vulnerability of the disciplined asceticism too easily yields to the comfortable and habitual tactics of devising ways to have an impact on another. We revert to staking a claim (and claiming a stake) in the other's life as a foothold for ourselves.

The pastoral counseling conversation is like no other conversation.

Or perhaps it is like the conversation God would have with us, the starkness of an honesty that is felt both as judgment and as grace just because it regards us as we are, an honesty empowered by a regard that is both utterly transcendent and intimately immanent.

Perhaps we can receive God's searing judgment, undefensively, constructively, because we recognize that it is not "personal." God is not settling personal grievances but persisting in acts of Creation. God's regard is so potent just because it is "without regard."

Perhaps God can be so intensely and graciously with us and for us that it feels safe and right to be honest just because God is, as we say, "above it all." God has nothing to prove, nothing to need, nothing at risk, so God can be unreservedly risky. God has nothing on the line, so God can put it all on the line.

The relationship is totally unlike a mutual romantic investment with its occasional wary maneuvers and gameplaying, bargaining timid disclosures for halting professions. With God we experience this curiously reassuring aloofness, this noninvolvement, as a guarantee that God's investment in our lives is firm, unreserved, unconditional.

And just as the transcendence confirms the immanence, so, too, the immanence reveals the transcendence; we come to feel God's presence so intensely and intimately with us that the experience transports. It feels "out of this world," and it is.

Perhaps the pastoral counseling relationship is like that. What the pastoral counselor provides is not a clever diagnosis, nor an astute remedy, nor a surfeit of love, but a constancy of attention, enabled by a disciplined abstinence from the vagaries of desire.

"Can You Talk with Me?"

Who is the counselee? Who is this person sitting here with you, in this unfamiliar posture of vulnerability? What brings someone to this strenuous, awkward, hopeful moment? What do you hear when I say, "Do you have some time to talk with me?" What is there in me that overcomes all my natural reserves of diffidence or pride and makes me risk the plea? What has induced me to step, falteringly, through the boundaries of our business as usual and into this alien moment of confessional?

These are not ordinary questions, and they invite more than ordinary discernment. As a counselor, your ears are tuned to hear things you don't hear in our business as usual. My trembling daring act of becoming a counselee calls you to step through boundaries, too, into the trembling daring act of becoming a counselor, into the discipline of according me an attentiveness more searing than either of us could withstand in our business as usual. As with others under religious discipline through the centuries, you let yourself be quietly focused on deeper essential meanings and undistracted by surface clutter.

So when I offer myself, tentatively, as counselee, you hear me confessing a woundedness I customarily hide—

and still want to hide even as I venture to disclose it—a depletion, paralysis, numbness. "I am not myself. I am beside myself. I am less than myself. I cannot see things as they are. I cannot feel things as they are. I cannot cope with things as I should. There is something wrong with me. I am broken. I am not as I was created to be. I need *help. I need* help. *I* need help."

It is to this sense of self-depletion and insufficiency, this sense of being a misfit and wrong that pastoral counseling is directed. Pastoral counseling aspires to a conversion, to a new sense of self, to an empowerment.

However casual the person is in lingering after a committee meeting or in crossing your path after worship, however businesslike or brazen or apologetic in claiming your time, however self-sufficient or even overbearing the person has always seemed to you, when you hear that phrase, "Can I talk to you?" or its equivalent, it should be taken as the self-disclosure of a tormented person who feels unable to cope. It's a cry for help that is more desperate than it may sound because it is a confession of some degree of personal deficiency and paralysis.

I feel transported into an alien world—that is the torment and the terror that brings me to pastoral counseling. I'm out of bounds, not in my familiar world, not in God's world. Either that or, as with Job, God has changed the rules. I am through the looking glass, into some parallel universe, where things don't work the way they should. Trust and faith are eroded, precarious, and hope and love sapped. A lifetime of verities is in question, in crisis. Like Job, I know in some residual but barely accessible place in my soul that I am all right. I'm not *really* crazy and helpless (or I would need more drastic therapy than pastoral counseling). I'm not *really* abandoned (or I would need more

drastic religious revival). I really *can* cope. I really *am* me. I
just can't cope, I can't feel myself, *here* and *now* and with *this*.
I can handle many things, but I can't handle *this*. T*his*
doesn't play by the rules. My usual strategies for dealing
with problems, the usual things I tell myself, and my usual
maneuvers with others don't work. I have plenty of reserves and resources. But they don't work this time. If the
usual worked, I wouldn't be here. For now I feel kidnapped
into another world, a demonic underworld, an alien other-
world. My life has been overpowered by invading aliens. I
have been conquered by a new strain of virus. I have lep-
rosy of the soul. I no longer fit into my own life. I don't know
how to live my life. This is the terror and the despair that
brings me to pastoral counseling. I am not myself.

SELF-ANXIETY CODED
AND PROTECTED BY "PROBLEMS"

The counselee cannot say such things at first, maybe not
for a long while. The counselor may or may not sense the
contours of this counselee's particular distress. The counselor doesn't need to. It is enough to know that the person
is asking for counseling to surmise that he or she feels apprehensive, overwhelmed, drowning, disabled, derailed.

You can hardly expect the counselee to portray and
name the distress clearly. The counselee is here precisely
because perspective and clarity are lost. Events are somehow out of focus, out of control. You will not be surprised,
or annoyed, when the counselee can't describe the problem in a way you can understand, or even when the counselee goes mute and unexpressive, or floods an hour with
rambling incoherence, or obsesses about circumstances
that are actually settled or resolved, or overreacts, or

seems blind to the obvious. If people could function well as counselees, they wouldn't be seeking counseling. In these "anticounseling" maneuvers, you will detect hints of what brings the person to counseling, overtones of feeling overwhelmed, incapacitated, disabled. You will realize that the counselee's core terror is that there is no core, that there is no one there, long before the counselee says it.

The counselee will speak at first, and perhaps at length, of events and circumstances and other people: a spouse's death, a lost job, a feared divorce, a mounting debt, a rebellious teenager, an abusive or uncommunicative mate, an injustice in the workplace, an unrelenting addiction, an invading tumor, or perhaps much less dramatic, the perplexities and quandaries of daily life. Murray speaks of Sam. Alice speaks of cleaning and landscaping and choosing highway routes. These events and circumstances are distressing, and the counselor will not disregard them or think them trivial. But they are not the business of counseling; they are the business of life. They may well be the business of the parish community and of the pastor as leader of this community, but they are not the business of pastoral counseling. These are things one talks about with friends, neighbors, lawyers, doctors, social workers, legislators, union leaders, or bartenders. They are problems that friends and neighbors—or professional experts—can help to resolve or try to. But not a counselor. What brings someone to counseling, and what counseling can deal with, are not the events and circumstances, but the wounds they inflict or disclose, their attack on the selfhood, the awful feelings they arouse of being incapacitated, unable to cope, alienated.

To be sure, the counselor, like the counselee, is tempted to focus on the outer events and circumstances, because they seem so much more tractable and manageable, as well as, at first glance, more compelling. But the counselor who intervenes and manages or resolves the circumstantial problem hijacks the opportunity for pastoral counseling. Such intervention not only fails the opportunity for enablement but in fact imposes further disempowerment by making the counselee feel all the more inept. To avoid this, the counselor offers, as a gift, the discipline of tolerating ambiguity and irresolution.

When the external circumstances are overwhelming—as in the experience of serious poverty or a massively abusive relationship—when life cannot be lived until some action is taken to deal with the circumstances, it is especially important to preserve the focus of pastoral counseling: the empowerment of the person. When circumstances are overwhelming, it is particularly tempting to see things in reverse, to suppose that these circumstances must be repaired before a person can benefit from counseling. But, in fact, when circumstances are overwhelming, the intentions of pastoral counseling are all the more urgent: to mobilize and empower the person to cope, to discern and take responsibility, to decide and enact changes and repairs.

Pastoral counseling deals with the meaning that the events have for the counselee. The work of pastoral counseling is to explore and expand the meaning the counselee finds in the events. Pastoral counseling aims at the disclosure of self, not the closure of a problem.

"I am not myself. I can't make it." These confessions are hard to make to friends and neighbors, and harder for them to accept. They are hard for a counselor to hear too; the counselor may wish he or she could be talking about events, circumstances, and other people, about facts rather than feelings. But these difficult confessions are what counseling is for.

A pastor is a pastor in many ways, all valid and important, all faithful to call and commission, sometimes relying on resources of theological perspective or of ordination, sometimes not. Sometimes a pastor exhorts and instructs, sometimes not. Sometimes a pastor intervenes, like any other good friend, to add resources to solving a problem, to finding a job, to making a decision, to breaking an addiction, to corralling stray passions. Sometimes, that is, a pastor works on the problem.

But sometimes a pastor is a counselor, and that is different.

As counselor, the pastor abstains from "working on the problem" for the sake of attending to the meaning the counselee attaches to these events. As counselor, the pastor is under the discipline of abstaining from the ordinary response to others' problems in order to deal with the extraordinary and less obvious dimensions. This approach requires discipline because these more direct and more obvious modes of helping are also the more familiar, more comfortable, and more satisfying modes. (What the pastor does *not* abandon, what makes *pastoral* counseling pastoral, is the vocation of holding another's life closely before God and of invoking God's presence in that life. It is just that the forms of that vocation may be different in counseling than the pastor is used to in other roles. We'll talk more about this later.)

In the counselee's life, distressing outer events have transmuted into internal distress. A death, a rejection, a failure, a quandary has left one feeling shriveled and stuck, poisoned and poisonous, helpless and hopeless, angry and self-blaming, empty of faith and trust. Sometimes the pastor finds ways to assault and assuage this inner distress, to correct the distorted views and doubts, to comfort.

But, again, sometimes a pastor is a counselor, and that is different.

As counselor, the pastor doesn't try to conquer the inner distress but nurtures it, trusts it as a necessary process that is gift and not curse, a part of Creation, not of the Fall. The counselor does not try to rescue the counselee from the valley of despair but walks with the counselee through this valley to see what can be found there. Faith comes not by denying the doubt but by wrestling with it. Hope is restored in facing the bleakness, love by living through the loneliness.

The pastoral counselor "accepts" the distress and its distortions not out of a permissive, sentimental compromise with principles but out of a firm commitment to the principle that God has chosen and provided the griefs and torments of life as a special mode of revelation and redemption.

Counseling is intended not to hear the report "I have problems" but to receive the confession "I feel like I *am* a problem." When the counselee's self-perception is converted back to "I *have* problems" (and "I have the resources to deal with them"), then counseling has done its work. If counseling begins with "Help, I'm in deep water so I must be drowning," it ends with "Look, I'm in deep water so I must be swimming." The counselor has enabled this outcome, not by dramatic rescue from the water or even by giving swimming lessons (though a pastor may sometimes, in noncounseling roles, perform the equivalent of rescue or lessons) but rather by swimming alongside. That is pastoral counseling.

HEARING THE MEANING
OF EVENTS AND PROBLEMS

The despair may indeed be occasioned by events, and the counseling may indeed begin with a recital of facts and events. But what the counselee brings to pastoral counseling are the wounds—the feelings of being impaired, overwhelmed, unable, the measure of oneself as small, as wanting, as alienated, alienated above all from oneself, the feelings of being kidnapped from one's own life, sidetracked, out of bounds, shipwrecked, derailed. What the counselee needs from the counseling is nothing more than a kind of personal conversion, a reorientation of self that restores wholeness and hope. And nothing less than that.

The usual doesn't work. So, in counseling, the counselee comes to feel safe enough to be willing to let go of the usual, to become naked of the familiar resources and strategies so as to discover new ways of coping, new things to tell the self and others. To deal with the distress, the counselee must become, in some sense, a child again, must relinquish hard-won and comfortable but failing patterns of identity and adulthood, and move for a time without moorings or maps. Pastoral counseling aims to make this risk possible.

COUNSELEE AS GRIEVER

Grief as Religious Confession

Pastoral counseling is the arena for wrestling with the fundamental religious confrontation between profoundly immortal hopes and stubbornly mortal limitations. That is, pastoral counseling is the arena for wrestling with grief. Perhaps we should always understand the counselee as a person in grief. Whatever a counselee's circumstances, whatever other emotions may be in the overtones, it may always be safe to perceive "Do you have time to talk?" as the signal that you are in the presence of grieving, a time for religious confession and growth. Something needful is missing and irrecoverable. Something especially relied on has proved mortal. The props are knocked out, and I am shattered. Perhaps something (spouse, marriage, job, public image, nimbleness of mind, suppleness of healthy body) in which I have invested myself, something I have made a foundation for my soul, has crumbled or disappeared, and I am desolate. It feels as though what I have lost is a part of myself, a central part. It feels that way because that is the way it is. We know ourselves in relationships and in our doings, and when a relationship is lost or the doings stymied, for a time, we cannot find ourselves. The inner progress of the soul has come to a crippling dead end, and the sense of self is devastated, all because something self and soul have relied on is not there. Grief brings one starkly to the archetypal religious confession that those things on which we commonly and inevitably rely to save us (status, work, spouses, children, wealth, etc.) are but fallible idols.

The numbing grief of the self forsaken also bares the frightening grief of the self insufficient. It is not only that an *other* on which I have relied has proved fallible; more excruciatingly, something *inner* on which I have relied has proved fallible. My desperate need to feel in command of my own destiny—and the illusion that I do—has been assaulted. Grief brings one starkly to the archetypal religious confession that the self cannot save itself.

So the angers and fears, the remorse and chagrin, the despair and the fertile vulnerability of grief are the ingredients of pastoral counseling. How *can* I be saved? Who will rescue me from this legacy of death? All grief counseling is pastoral counseling. All pastoral counseling is grief counseling.

Grief of the Finished and Unfinished

There are two kinds of grief: the grief over what is finished and the grief over what is unfinished. The grief of a past that must stay in the past, forever gone; and the grief of a future that must stay in the future, perpetually beyond. The grief of "once more" becoming "never again"; and the grief of "not yet" becoming "never." The grief to which the resurrection is the response of faith; and the grief to which eschatological hope is the response.

The first grief—the sorrow over what is now finished—is the more familiar. It is what is usually meant by "grief." It is the more assuagable. In facing retirement, Murray grieves the loss of status and satisfaction that work brings him. In facing her father's decline, Alice grieves the loss of a vigorous parent. The past is gradually left behind, and one moves on.

The second grief—the pang over what is destined to remain unfinished—haunts unremittingly. What might have been, what should have been, remains just that. Unkept promises remain promises still unkept—those promises made to me, which I have trusted, and, still more excruciatingly, those promises I have made to others, which I thought I meant. For Murray it is facing the fact that work will never provide for him the satisfactions he always dreamed of. Alice will never have the relationship with her father that she yearns for. Something that still needs to happen will never happen.

Conventional grief counseling deals with endings, with what is finished: a marriage, a career, a parent's life (or the idealization of spouse, career, or parent). It remembers and celebrates what has been and lets it be finished. The album and diary entries are savored, one by one, and the page is turned. Memories are consigned to be memories. With or without explicit pastoral counseling, the grief work will happen.

Still, when a spouse dies, or the ending comes to any other portion of life, not only is there the searing grief of the finished but also the haunting grief of the unfinished: things deferred, things unsaid, intimacies still unexchanged. The easier grief of the finished may disturb the repose of the self, but the griefs of the unfinished erode the worth of the self, and so especially command the attention of the pastoral counselor.

The grief of the unfinished appears not just in the acute moments of death, loss, and change. It is a chronic, persistent, low-grade, disconsolate nagging at the soul of the faithful. Such grief is the substance of pastoral counseling because it is the brooding shadow that always accompanies faith, hope, and love, the substance of all pastoral care. Faith, hope, and love, the promises we exchange with God, bid us to a life beyond our own. So the aspiration exalts our life but also dooms us to the despair of chasing what is beyond our reach. Promises that lofty must forever remain promises. That is their purpose, and that is their curse. If the aspirations of faith, hope, and love have already brought a person into pastoral care, into a pastor's community, then the grief-stricken partialness of faith, hope, and love will bring that person to the doorstep of pastoral counseling.

Those less well endowed (it is tempting to say less afflicted by) with faith, hope, and love are more immune to grief. Those with the highest aspirations to the religious virtues are most vulnerable to the despair of grief. It is the religious heroes taking massive gulps of faith, hope, and love who become tragic heroes, completely enveloped in what cannot sustain. "I poured my soul upon the sand," Augustine lamented (Book 4 of his Confessions). "He whom I loved as though he would never die was dead." Strong faith, strong hope, strong love cannot but pour itself out, prodigally and recklessly, and cannot but issue in strong grief.

Grief, then, is the badge of one committed to the unattainable imperatives and promises that transcend, undergird, define—and thwart—the self. Grief is the badge of membership in a community of faithful aspirers. Grief is the mark of one who has been vouchsafed a glimpse of the promised land and so cannot but live in it even while unable to live in it. Daily life can never be the same again, never dreary and meaningless, because it is now lived in the transcendent hope, but also never without a twinge of melancholy because it is now lived in the transcendent hope.

The pastoral counselor, vicar of the community of those enlivened and tormented by hope, knows well this blessing and this torment—nowhere more than in the act of pastoral counseling. As we shall see in chapter 3, the counselor's role is that of witnessing and re-visioning the life of the counselee in light of the realities of the faith, hope, and love, which are the counselee's lot. But the counselor's burden is to sense these aspirations so keenly as to be excruciatingly aware of how the counselee's life (like the counselor's counseling) falls short. That burden keeps the counselor in constant temptation to intervene, to reduce the counselor's discomfort over the dissonance by maneuvering the counselee's life into conformity with the mandates and promises of the transcendent. However, the counselor resists the temptation to live the counselee's life and remains faithful to the commitment to provide the context that will enable the counselee to live his or her own life faithfully in a way that embraces the grief.

LOCATING COUNSELING IN THE COUNSELEE'S LIFE

To be more formal about locating pastoral counseling in the counselee's life, we can distinguish four "levels" or facets of human development. All clamor for attention; however, not all are equally appropriate for the pastoral counselor to attend to. We can diagram the levels and their relationship:

Context→Self-Regard→Traits and Habits→Coping and Functioning

Coping and Functioning

This is the realm of everyday behavior in which I count my successes and failures. I do my work, relate to others, live my faith, meet my responsibilities as a citizen, get my priorities straight, grieve my losses, and confront adversity and adversaries. I do these things well or not so well, and I try to do them better. They are most likely to be exactly and explicitly what I talk about when I come to counseling ("Things are not going well on the job, or at home, or in my retirement," etc.). The counselor considers this the vocabulary of the *presenting* problem and knows there are overtones yet to be sounded and heard. But the counselee and friends and family are likely to think of the presenting problem as *the* problem. "My boss is being unfair to me. I am not relating well to my kids. I don't have my old zest for helping in the day care. I want to change these behaviors. I want to cope better, to function better. Others want me to change these behaviors, and they are ready to tell me how." Offering advice on such practical matters may be extremely useful. But this is *not* the realm of pastoral counseling. The pastoral counselor may be extremely tempted, sometimes for very attractive and valid reasons (and sometimes for less worthy reasons), to intervene into a counselee's life at this level and to work on changes in behavior, to teach how to cope, how to function, to make an immediate and direct difference. But this is not the business of pastoral counseling. Improved functioning is, of course, to be fondly welcomed when it happens, and, in a sense, can even be regarded as a long-range goal of pastoral counseling. But it is a goal to be achieved indirectly, as a by-product, not something to be produced by pastoral counseling. ("Producers" stage shows or manage factories; neither is a suitable model for pastoral counseling.)

Traits and Habits—Personality Characteristics

In the perpetual fencing match with the world, which describes everyone's normal process of development, the self thrusts and parries, ventures and retreats, feints and dodges, and gradually perfects certain strategies for being in the world—we call them personality characteristics, traits, or talents—that seem to keep the path relatively smooth and safe.

Problems in coping and functioning are seldom isolated. They are parts of more general patterns. The breakdown in relations with a boss turns out to be similar to a breakdown in relations with a previous boss, and/or a spouse, and/or a parent, and/or loss of faith. Seeing the pattern helps to focus and define the issues with the boss. It also defuses and diffuses tension with this particular person by attending to the more general pattern or *trait*. Colloquially, this is the "baggage" one brings to a squabble.

Discerning such patterns is often thought to be the mission and the skill of all mental health professionals (a category in which pastoral counseling may sometimes be included—erroneously, I think). ("You hate/fear your boss/God/therapist/spouse because/as you hated/feared your father.") A therapist is thought to be like a detective solving a mystery by finding the early clues that "explain" later events, or the traits (always "underlying" traits) that "explain" behaviors. It's a challenge or a game bested by astute wits and insight, an intellectual contest.

In the contemporary culture that prizes such psychological savvy, counselees and their friends and pastoral counselors also are likely to be intrigued by and even adept at this kind of psychologizing, the finding of general patterns of behavior. Such skill, providing it is chastened, disciplined, and responsible—that is, providing it is accurate—is usually welcomed. It yields vocabulary and analytic insight that may become useful tools. But it should never be mistaken for either the means or the ends of pastoral counseling. For one thing, pastoral counseling is not an intellectual exercise that whets psychological cleverness, but more of an affective experience that embraces the whole person. For another, traits—whether benign or otherwise—and talents—whether sturdy or otherwise—do not emerge from, and are seldom modified by, intellectual awareness and insight. Naming a pattern is satisfying but seldom improves it.

Traits and talents are not modules of machinery to be turned on or off, inserted or modified or otherwise engineered. They are organic growths, and they grow out of the interaction between an emerging selfhood and its environment. Throughout its lifetime of development, the self learns to deal with the world of reality in ways that assert, gratify, protect, and defend the self by devising and adopting a variety of strategies and postures. These strategies and postures are what we refer to as traits and talents. We can understand them and we can affect them not by regarding them as autonomous, but as emerging out of complex developmental processes. These processes must be affected if we are to influence the traits and talents that govern coping and functioning. So we turn to the next "level" of development.

Self–Regard

In the process of growing a personality and its traits, nothing is more important than self-regard, the way the self perceives itself. Does the self feel safe or threatened, large or small, sturdy or fragile, vivid or shadowy, true or false, integrated or divided, available and present or hidden and obscure? If I feel myself unsafe or inadequate, for example, I will adopt strategies that exaggerate aggressiveness, rigidity, or defensiveness at the cost of underdeveloping strategies of fluidity or smooth interaction with others. If I feel safe, sturdy, and together, I will venture strategies that stretch the self, extend it beyond narrow boundaries into more intimate liaisons with events and people. In terms of the diagram, high regard for self fosters traits and talents that function well and cope well.

The counselee recognizes the crucial importance of self-regard, and its occasional fragility, when he or she remarks, "I don't feel myself these days" or "I don't know just where I fit in" or "I just don't want to get out of bed these days." Or the counselee may tote up the impact of pastoral counseling by noticing "I feel better about myself" rather than just "I feel friendlier or more comfortable or more peaceful" (traits and talents) or "My spouse and I are getting along better" (coping and functioning).

This level of self-regard can be an arena for the functioning of God's grace. It occasions the kinds of affirmations—about "being"—that we associate with the power of grace. The level of functioning and even the level of traits invite the kinds of appraisals and admonitions— about "doings"—that we associate with the workings of law.

Far more than the levels of coping and functioning or of traits and habits, the level of self-regard *is* the business of pastoral counseling. The pastoral counselor knows that difficulty in coping and awkwardness of trait reflect something askew in self-regard. The pastoral counselor knows that an enhanced self-regard can be trusted to discover improved traits and to devise more effective functioning. Whether or not they are ever discussed in counseling, the traits and the coping benefit from the enhanced self-regard, which *is* addressed by the counselor.

Enabling self-regard is indirect. It's an art not a science; an experience not an instruction. Acquiring and mastering this art is the discipline of pastoral counseling. Self-regard cannot be engineered or manufactured; it cannot be willed or talked into being. Self-regard grows, like all else in Creation, when given a chance, when provided a benign and nurturing environment. So for the clearest and most compelling sense of its mission, pastoral counseling turns to a fourth level of human development.

Pastoral Counseling

Context

We all live evicted from that Garden which is created just for us, and so we cannot escape some degree of that wariness and wiliness which we require to survive outside the garden but which stunts our hearty growth. The self can survive and thrive only when it can trust, and outside the garden, trust is jaded. At best, then, we are distorted and dysfunctional—sinners, we used to say, and perhaps still should. Some portions, some moments of our lives are afflicted with a threat and sense of fragility, so at these times our energies are especially distracted into defensive strategizing, squandered on building fences rather than bridges. We may protect ourselves, but we don't function well. One does not move nimbly or gracefully while wearing heavy armor, whether metallic or psychological.

Pastoral counseling cannot change the basic realities of the context in which we have lived and do live. It cannot remove whatever threats and disdain have plagued us, whatever bribes, whatever tightly conditioned love and respect. It cannot make the context in which we find, or try to find, ourselves more benign than it is. (God doesn't do that either. God doesn't save us by removing curses and sin, but in spite of them, by blunting the power they hold over us, by offering a radically new experience of grace, a new context.)

Pastoral counseling cannot change reality. But it can offer a time-out from struggling with hostile contexts, and it can offer a sample of a more benign reality. For a few minutes, now and then, we can begin to let down our guard, take off our armor, and see what it is like to channel our energies not into protecting ourselves but into productive, constructive, creative adventure. (We'll talk more about this process in the coming chapters.) Here, the point is to locate pastoral counseling, to notice that the level of *context* is where pastoral counseling aims to make a difference. The pastoral counselor does not aim directly to change styles of coping and functioning, to revise personality traits, or to improve self-regard. The pastoral counselor does try to offer a graceful context, trusting that this will in turn impact the self-regard, personality traits, and modes of functioning.

A fifth level? Perhaps that last statement leaves too much initiative and responsibility to the pastoral counselor. In fact, the counselor does not generate this gracious context but simply communicates it. Changes in coping and personal functioning all depend on a benign context provided by the pastoral counseling. But *that* depends on something too: the prior experience by the counselor of grace. The counselor cannot deliver what the counselor has not received. So a fifth level of experience assumed in this analysis is the pastoral counselor's own experience of blessing.

Which brings us to a confession at the heart of pastoral counseling. This healing never happens as neatly or thoroughly as we would like to depict it. Pastoral counselors are highly imperfect vessels of grace. Our own sense of participating in a "benign context" is ambiguous and partial, at best, and therefore so is our capacity to convey such an experience to others. If pastoral counseling proceeded at the level of coping, we might easily fall victim to the pretense of expertise and let ourselves believe that we could correctly coach and prescribe how to deal, for example, with a difficult boss. People do let themselves fantasize such expertise, and that is one of the urgent problems in conducting counseling addressed to that level. But when we recognize that the key, the germ of counseling is lodged in the experience of grace, we readily acknowledge how flawed and imperfect is our own spiritual journey—a confession that opens us and our pastoral counseling more fully to the influx of grace that is essential to its effectiveness.

IN SUMMARY

What brings someone to pastoral counseling? Who is the counselee? What is the agenda for pastoral counseling?

The vocabulary of the counseling may be an array of problems, events, situations, relationships, daily behaviors—circumstances about the counselee's life that need adjusting The vocabulary of the counseling may even include strategies for making these adjustments. But the agenda for the pastoral counseling has to do with the meaning these circumstances have for the counselee.

The counselor may safely expect to hear something like this as the meaning, the agenda:

My life is wrong. It is not the life I was promised. It is not the life I have promised. It is not the life that was intended for me. It is not the life that I intended. I am not myself. I need conversion. I need to be re-deemed. How can I be saved?

I am not living my own life. I feel fractured, sidelined, out of the action of my own life. I feel like a spectator to my own life, alienated from myself. I need integration, integrity. How can I become whole, healed, holy?

My life is beyond my control. I don't know how to live my life. I can't cope. I am baffled, vexed. I have resources, but they don't work anymore. I need empowerment.

How can I be graced?

"Can You Talk with Me?"

My life seems subject to unfriendly forces, not just alien but hostile. A spiritual virus is eroding my soul. Things don't play by the rules anymore. They call forth my worst. They drive me into desperate, defensive maneuvers that thwart and twist and distort. I need trust and peace. How can I recover faith, hope, and love?

These are the fundamental and familiar spiritual torments that make pastoral counseling *pastoral*. Addressing these torments is the tacit commitment of both counselor and counselee. What makes pastoral counseling *counseling* is that these questions are incarnated in daily events and life problems and are addressed in the vocabulary of those events and problems. Counselor and counselee seldom speak of their commitments and goals in the familiar but abstract language used in the above paragraphs; they encode these existential issues in the vocabulary of daily events. The discipline required of the pastoral counselor is to maintain fidelity to the fundamental spiritual goals while acknowledging the authority of the incarnated form in which they are presented.

The Counselee's
Experience of Counseling

How does it feel to be a counselee? How do counselees describe the experience of pastoral counseling?

It is usually startling, a strenuous adjustment, hard to describe, hard to get used to. It is a culture shock. It is like landing in an alien culture where social conventions are different, where people behave differently from what you expect, where people treat you differently from what you are used to. It's not an unpleasant change, but it is nevertheless abrupt and jarring. The ways of behaving that make you who you are—your self-defining, self-defending, self-enhancing habits of personality—don't work well and are not called for.

Maybe it is as startling and as freeing as learning to survive the dust, heat, thirst, and vastness of the desert and then suddenly finding yourself in an oasis where life is not fragile but abundant and assured, so that all your habitual survival skills are useless and unnecessary. As delightful as the change may be, it still leaves you psychologically naked. Maybe it is like having to shift from the well-practiced strategizing of courting a lover to the experience of feeling securely and unconditionally loved, and, in doing so, finding oneself speechless and helpless. Maybe it is like breaking out of everyday experience for a moment of glimpsing the kingdom—surrendering to one's most daring yearning for an untroubled, relaxed, unguarded, healing moment—a glimpse afforded us, we are told, only if we are able to become childlike.

It takes some getting used to. It takes some time to trust. The counselor has stepped out of everyday life into this deliberately different and transcending world as an act of discipline (to be discussed more fully in the next chapter). For the counselee, it is an act of discovery.

Words fail because words are the creatures (and creators) of everyday experience. The yearnings and needs that the counseling milieu meets are largely unspoken, and so is their realization. We have words for the coping and functioning end of the sequence diagrammed in the last chapter (which is where counselees usually expect counseling to be located), but not for the context end (where the counseling turns out to be located). Counselees turn to imagery and analogy to convey the experience of pastoral counseling.

"I felt freer, more myself," is the most common report. "I could take off masks, armor, stop pretending, stop trying to impress. I stopped worrying about whether I was pleasing or displeasing my counselor, stopped calculating things to say that would woo her and win her."

"I didn't feel constantly challenged. I didn't feel the need to be always vigilant, on guard, proving myself, protecting myself from being put down. I didn't feel at risk."

"Paradoxically, my pastoral counselor somehow became invisible, a non-factor in my life, even while he loomed huge, pervasive. He wasn't a player, but he was a presence."

It is like a sanctuary, one says, a wildlife sanctuary where life can go on naturally as it is supposed to, without fear of the depredations of "civilization."

"And if 'sanctuary' means a holy place, I guess that's a good definition of holy—a freedom to be yourself as created by God, undistorted by the fear of hostile trespassers. People sometimes use the church as sanctuary from persecution by political authorities. I think I used pastoral counseling as sanctuary from persecution by other authorities in my life. Calling it a sanctuary recognizes a power in my life higher than the people I am running away from."

The counselee can experience a time-out, a time-off, can go off-duty. It's not an escape from problems and responsibilities. These things remain, but for the moment they are not sovereign; they are not defining or demanding your life. It's a moratorium from the pressure to perform, to conquer the problems, to appease all the responsibilities. It's a few minutes in which no one is keeping score, in which it doesn't matter whether you surmount the problems or succumb to them. Are the problems and responsibilities more than you can handle? Who cares right now? There is nothing at stake, nothing at risk in your present relationship with the person you are talking with, your pastoral counselor.

"In the counseling, I became heedless of other people—and I also became more mindful of other people, heedless of others as shapers of my life and mindful of others as opportunities in my life."

Does pastoral counseling displace or replace other relationships in the counselee's life? Does the counselor become a substitute for other important people? Does the counselee "fall in love" with the counselor, forsaking "real life" loves? Sometimes this happens, but it is not an intended effect of pastoral counseling. It can be minimized by the counselor's disciplined abstinence from affect (see next chapter). It is a distortion that counseling itself should correct. More often counselees report a curious paradox about how they feel about other people while they are talking with the counselor. On the one hand, the dealings with others seem more remote, less intense, less urgent ("I don't need to have that showdown with her."). On the other hand, people feel closer, more real, more present; relationships feel warmer.

The time-out is like a truce, says a man whose troubled marriage prompted him and his wife to seek pastoral counseling. "Like joking about the game with the other team during a football time-out, or like they told about troops in World War I coming out of the trenches and having a Christmas party together. It seemed like a time when there was no point in my wife and I shooting at each other, so we tried something else."

One counselee said that the experience of counseling was like being relieved for an afternoon of the constant care of an invalid mother. She was free to nap, shop, scrub the kitchen floor, consult a doctor about her mother—all without having the constant fear of missing her mother's call, of not giving the medications properly, of not making her comfortable, of displeasing her. Perhaps it is even more like the experience of being assisted in the caretaking by someone who is without the personal stake, who does not panic or scold or reassure, who is not terror-struck about pleasing or discomforting mother.

Another counselee described the climate of pastoral counseling this way: "It's like the time last winter when my car stalled, and I couldn't get it going again. Everyone behind me started honking, and everyone around me stared, and I found myself trying to deal with them more than with the car, and I wasn't doing very well with either. Then I saw this big cop ambling over to me, and I really panicked: Now

I'm going to get a ticket for obstructing traffic. I fumbled with the window—one more thing I couldn't manage well. Then he leaned nonchalantly on the car, grinned, and finally said, 'These Corollas just don't like this weather; it happens all the time.' Then he ambled away saying, 'I guess I'll go see what they are making all that noise about.' He meant, 'Don't let them bother you.' And they didn't and I calmed down, remembered to tap the gas pedal, and got the car going. He made a place for me where the pressure and self-consciousness and demands were off."

It's a shelter for the homeless, one person has said, the spiritually homeless. It gets you off the streets psychologically and gives you the spiritual equivalent of a good night's rest and a good meal.

"I feel like my pastoral counselor is the one person in my life who doesn't have a claim on me. Everyone else wants something from me—or sometimes what is worse, they want something for me—and I spend all my energy fending them off or compromising or explaining so as not to antagonize them—except when I explode and blow up. But I don't have to do this with her."

Pastoral counseling has been likened to gulping a breath of fresh air after being trapped under water or in a stuffy room or in a cloud of smog. Sometimes one doesn't recognize the smog as smog or its poisoning effects until one tastes the fresh air. Or perhaps it is like catching your breath after losing it in the panicked panting of fright, flight, or fight.

Pastoral counseling provides a *virtual* life-space. You can practice living. But the risks are confined to the simulation. You can always reset and try again. It's a training module in which you are guaranteed a safe landing.

"It is the opposite of all the warnings about 'driving

defensively,' which have pretty much preoccupied and preempted my life."

"Driving defensively" means to expect the worst at all times from all people. It means to be attentive to the dangers that may loom at any time without warning. It means to stay on duty and not be distracted by leisurely sightseeing. It means to learn to read the most subtle signs of lurking disaster—the child on the sidewalk looking at the street, the car ahead changing lanes, the slight tug of a softening tire. It means to take the responsibility for averting trouble, even though the trouble may be started by someone else. It means, above all, constantly adjusting your own driving to meet and forestall all possible threats. Your driving is governed by the threats. Safety First is the rule; everything else takes a back seat. The defensive driver renounces conversation, companionship, scenery, radio, even destination (in the sense that getting there safely becomes more important than the "there"). That could be the slogan by which most of us live our lives, whether or not we are in a car: "Drive defensively."

Imagine what it would feel like to cruise the highway with safety somehow guaranteed, to drive without the need to be defensive. Just for this trip, you can be assured of no surprise ice spots, no errant drivers, no tire defects. You *can* be on vacation and enjoy the scenery, your companion, and your driving because you don't need to marshal all energies into defending. Relaxing, stretching the mind, freeing the spirit, discovering what it's like to be a different person, a nondefensive driver—or even a passenger—these new adventures may take a little practice. But the moratorium on risk is ample enough for that.

That's how it must feel to enter the temporary safety of counseling. The risks are abated. You can relax the lifelong habits of living defensively, of putting all energies into survival, of adjusting yourself to avert trouble. You can practice living as you choose, not living on perpetual guard duty.

Counseling, of course, is artificial, a *virtual* road trip. It's not a real car on a real road in real traffic; no one can pretend to guarantee real life from harm. But in the training module, you can practice real driving under guaranteed safety.

You don't need to squander your energies in the repertory of preemptive self-justifications at which you are so practiced, because, for just this moment at least, no one is judging or keeping score; no one is responding to you with lurking appraisals of good or bad, yes or no. There is no need to protect, pretend, strut, or hide. You can find out what's there, what's possible, what's wanted behind the defensive facades and charades.

THE DIFFERENCE DEFINED

Pastoral counseling, then, provides an atmosphere, an emotional climate, a temporary virtual reality that the counselee usually experiences as different from everyday life in at least two crucial ways. First, the counselee is dealing with a person, the counselor, who looms in the counselee's life as a large presence, but not as a player. The counselee does not have to negotiate with the counselor as an adviser, as a coach, or as one who in any other way proffers an agenda or prescription. So the counselee can feel like a person, not a player. It's a moratorium on submitting the self to the buffeting of everyday life. The counselor is largely indifferent to the hassles, decisions, and dilemmas that seemed to beset the counselee to the point of seeking counseling. The counselor is not trying to "do" anything, so the counselee can just "be." Second, though the counseling relationship may be without agenda or prodding, it is not without affect. The counselor is experienced in affording personal support and regard that is unwavering and intimate. Because the counselor offers no agenda, no checklist, no criteria, that regard is felt as unconditional.

A Presence, Not a Player

Pastoral counseling provides an encounter, an atmosphere. We refer to the diagram that structured the last chapter and emphasize here that the pastoral counseling intervenes at the context end of the sequence, not the coping end. The counselee enters the pastoral counseling at the right end of the diagram but experiences the impact of the counseling at the left end.

The counselee arrives at counseling telling of events, circumstances, or persons that he or she defines as the problem. This is what needs changing. The conversation begins with talk about job or spouse or disease, and the vocabulary may even remain there; the counseling may end with the conversation still apparently about job or spouse or disease. Indeed the counseling, one hopes, improves the way these concerns are fit into the counselee's life. But the counseling is not about these matters. The counselor has not attended, primarily, to them. The effect of the counseling, the impact the counselee experiences, is in another domain.

In the beginning, if the counselee speaks of self, it is usually a self that is identified with these "problems," a self that is defined by them. Who am I? I am the victim, the culprit, or the dunce caught up in this turmoil. The self is rooted in the domain of coping because the domains at the left end of the diagram have atrophied. There is little sense of self as such because there is so little sense of a sustaining defining context. The sense of self is limited to the arena of coping and its failures in that arena, narrowed as though an actor on the stage had no sense of self beyond the twists of plot he or she was assigned to pursue for a couple of hours, no sense of self to bring to curtain calls or a life offstage, as though the only way to behave at the cast party is to perpetuate the onstage struggles.

The pastoral counseling offers the counselee grounds for a selfhood independent of the coping problems, because the counselor is a presence independent of them and wants to regard the counselee as a person independent of them.

In the grounding, the counselee experiences a freshening, an energizing, and a wholing (=*healing* =*holying*) of person. There is a conversion of self from feeling some version of "I am a lost sinner" to feeling some version of "I am a lost sinner who also lives in God's grace." The counseling does not change the coping problems; they persist. The counseling does not—necessarily or immediately—change the ways the counselee addresses these problems, or even the way the counselee feels about them—the problems are still harrowing and baffling. The pastoral counseling does change the way the counselee feels about himself or herself. This proves the crucial difference. It proves to be the context that enables the counselee to muster the resources and skills to address or withstand the "problem."

This is how and why pastoral counseling is and must be different from other types of counseling. Friends and family respond to a problem or a crisis with advice and assistance in the coping. "Have you tried . . . ? Can I do anything? When that happened to me, I . . . You'll get over it." Often such helpfulness is constructive, even crucial; that's what friends and families are for. They become deeply involved; they make your problem their problem and struggle to solve it with all the personal energy of their own investment. They want you to accept the gift of their solution.

Pastoral counseling is different. By disciplined intent, the counselor is not personally invested in the problem, does not make it his or her own problem, and so is not compelled or qualified to search for ways to solve it.

When the pastoral counselor violates this discipline and does struggle to find or coach solutions to the problems, pastoral counseling is jeopardized. In two ways the counseling is precluded from providing the experience of unconditioned regard and support for self, which is the mission and gift of counseling. First, it is an opportunity missed: attention to the "problems," the issues of coping, preempts attention to the self, which is in fact the far more urgent need of the counselee. Second, attention to the "problems," the issues of coping, keeps the conversation precisely in the domain that has most likely proved devastating. Most likely, it is in fending off a well-meaning parent or other coach that the counselee has felt battered, most reduced to bartering, when the self has felt most teased and most dazed with conditioned offers of esteem, has experienced the most panic in trying to meet conditions to earn some respect. It is precisely the coaching, advising, and "helping" in the past that have eroded the sense of selfhood and left selfhood and love dependent on futile struggles to measure up and warrant affection and esteem. The counselor seriously risks becoming one more dispenser of love in exchange for performance.

Unconditional Regard

Pastoral counseling assuages the pervasive human hunger for love without condition. In childhood and adulthood, most of us find ourselves required to barter for love and to earn, deserve, and win by our efforts and guardedness the esteem and affection without which we do not feel real or rooted. We are teased. We are tendered conditioned offers of love. The lover asks something from us in exchange. We are forced to focus our energies on the conditions, not on the love; on our own strategizing rather than on what we receive; on the means rather than the end. The anguish of misfitting the other's script and agenda supplants the delight of fitting into the other's life. The conditioned love compels us to live, as best we can, by our wits and wiliness—what Freud called our I—which is to say, by a distortion of our selfhood. But we are not created to live by our wits, by our I. We are created to live by our relationships and belonging, by faith, hope, and love. It is the conditioning of love that compels us to rely on our own strengths and therefore to carefully defend, exaggerate, and pretend such strength. It is the conditioning of love that compels us to deny and hide vulnerabilities, which is to deny the truth about ourselves. The conditioning compels us to pretend and defend self-sufficiency and to deny and prevent our dependence on others.

These distortions we impose on ourselves as part of our bartering tactics lead us into the dead ends of helplessness and hopelessness, the mistrust of self and of others, the problems and distress that bring us to pastoral counseling. In response, pastoral counseling provides surcease from the bartering and battering. It provides an alternative to the marketplace as the locus and the referee for the transaction of love. It provides corrective to the climate that has generated distortion and distress. Pastoral counseling provides a steady, unwavering regard that need not, that cannot, be manipulated; it is a regard that is not under the control of the counselee. "Whether or not I try to make it happen, this other is on my side, is with me."

The counselor's regard for the counselee does not substitute for the love of parent, spouse, child, or neighbor, which the counselee may have experienced only in rationed scarcity. It does not match in magnitude or salience the loves of real life. It is, to be sure, a common misunderstanding of counseling to suppose that the counselor does or should supply loving support so intense and intimate that it makes up for what has been missed and satisfies the hunger. When counselors seem to assume this burden or issue this promise, or when counselees summon this hope or issue this demand—that counselor can/must be God or parent—this is a distortion that itself deserves airing and remedy.

Pastoral counseling offers correction and remedy for the *conditioned quality* of crucial love in the counselee's past, not for the *diminished magnitude* of love. The counselor does not pretend to be God, parent, or spouse in prodigality of love. But whatever regard, esteem, or even love the counselor and counseling do offer the counselee, that *is* unconditional. The counselor has adopted the discipline of entering into an abstinent relationship in which he or she feels there is nothing at risk and nothing at stake, and in which there are no needs for personal satisfaction, no self-image to be guarded or bolstered, and no fragility to be protected. The counselor is immunized from being personally affected by anything the counselee says or does. The counselor's regard is unaffected, unresponsive, unconditional. If this seems like an artificially numb and one-sided relationship, it is. This is not a model or sample of how two people enter into intimate mutuality; it is a model of unconditional regard. The counselee is deprived of any leverage over the counselor, of any bargaining chips, and of anything with which to barter. The counselee has no way to seduce or enhance the counselor's regard, but also has no way to shrink or lose that regard. That regard is steady and unconditional, not because the counselor possesses any godlike power or virtue in loving, not because of any talent or skill in personal relationships, but because the counselor has been willing to accept the discipline of entering into an abstinent relationship and to renounce the satisfaction of personal needs. This immunizes the counselor's regard from conditions under the counselee's control.

This is often called "acceptance." But that is a misleading word if it implies approval or agreement or any other affective involvement by the counselor. The counselor's discipline of abstinence of affect means that his or her regard transcends questions concerning approval or endorsement. The counselor is abstracted into a situation of literally "not caring" what the counselee does or says while still unwaveringly caring for the counselee. The acceptance the counselee experiences is not approval or disapproval, not empathy or sympathy. It is not even tolerance or neutrality, for that would imply a personal affective reaction simply being withheld. The acceptance of the counselor is not a personal affective reaction. It is a stark, naked, existential, even depersonalized, regard of being. The counselor communicates a kind of sublimely nonchalant "whatever" about the counselee's doings while communicating a sublime unequivocal "yesness" about the counselee's personhood.

This is—to repeat the acknowledgment and caution— not an attractive model for human relationship. Pastoral counseling is not supposed to be such a model. It is not a friendship; it is not a paradigm for other forms of a pastoral relationship. Perhaps it can be said to resemble (and illuminate) the paradox of God's simultaneous transcendence and immanence, how God can be so intensely invested in human affairs yet remain so utterly abstracted and independent from them that God's gracious regard is unwaveringly immune to the ups and downs of those affairs. Perhaps the counselor's regard resembles the awesomely total welcome parents offer a newborn baby, totally affirming its very being without regard for any personal qualities or traits or behaviors, without regard for any virtue, skills, trespass, or failure—for there is none yet.

So the counselee does not experience intensely affective endorsement of behavior, opinions, or decisions. By the same token, the counselee experiences a starkly naked and utterly reliable affirmation that he or she is indeed a fully formed and legitimate human being, one entitled to walk this planet upright and to claim rights and responsibilities in God's Creation just as everyone else—despite any previous messages to the contrary.

Diverse Correctives for Diverse Deficits

As urgent as the hunger for unconditional love is for most of us, a caveat is called for here. Unconditional regard may not be everyone's most urgent hunger. For some it may not be the marketplacing of love that has rendered their lives fallen and distorted. There are other poisons abroad, such as violent assaults on body and spirit and denied accessibility to love and opportunity. Therefore, for some counselees, unconditional regard may not be the corrective most needed in pastoral counseling.

Most of the discussions in this book assume that the distortions and inner distresses that bring people to pastoral counseling are rooted in the dynamics of bartering for affection and esteem, a system of bartering that is imposed by the rationed and conditioned availability of love, a system of bartering that compels people to distort and constrict themselves as they maneuver to induce others to grant affection. Life is reduced to the dishonest scramble of a dating game. Pastoral counseling intends to address the distortions and distress by recognizing these roots and providing a sample of an alternative reality, an atmosphere that is safe because regard is steady, unwavering, not at risk, not conditioned, not vulnerable to the maneuvers, stratagems, and wooing of the counselee. The need most often addressed in pastoral counseling is the need for relief from the marketplacing and conditioning of love.

However, the need for unconditional regard is not absolute or universal. It is culturally relative. I believe it is the crucial developmental plight for most people likely to be reading this book and for most pastoral counselees they are likely to encounter. But not all. It is important not to absolutize or universalize this prescription of unconditional regard as a foundation of pastoral counseling and to be open to other needs for corrective alternative realities. When the deficits of life are different, pastoral counseling is called to intervene with different correction.

The bartering-for-love analysis may be most accurate as a portrayal of the developmental experience of male European-Americans and of a culture dominated by them. It is the white male and those especially influenced by him who may especially feel the urgency to have it all and who may regard all of reality as a reluctant lover to be seduced or a teasing lover to be tamed. Love is a commodity to be amassed, to be bought, to be fought for rather than a resource to be savored or a transcendent reality to be trusted and welcomed as a gift.

If pastoral counseling is or should be different for women or for African-Americans, this is the point at which the difference must take hold, in the understanding of this distinct developmental history. For any person, the question is, "What is the distinct context that has nurtured distortions and that now deserves the correction of a distinctly different pastoral counseling context?"

Perhaps some persons experience love not as a tease, conditionally and ambiguously present, but as massively blockaded and inaccessible, as by abuse or withholding. Such barriers induce the distortions not of bartering but of submission and resignation. The corrective context, then, would not be that of steady, unconditioned regard, but that of accessibility and insistence. It is not the masks of disguise that the counselee is induced to shed, but the heavy cowl of hiding and disappearance.

Welcoming the Difference

This chapter has emphasized, perhaps even exaggerated, the abrupt dissonance the counselee experiences between the attitude of the pastoral counselor and the attitudes conveyed in the noncounseling everyday world. There may even be startling dissonance between the attitudes conveyed by the pastor in counseling roles and those conveyed by the same pastor in noncounseling pastoral roles.

The difference is restorative and healing, but it may also be troubling, especially at first. The counselor may seem unaccountably indirect, indifferent, withholding, absent, evasive, disinterested in the immediate, urgent problems that beset the counselee, unopinionated about questions on which the counselee expects the pastor to be expert. The distance between a counselor located at the left end of the diagram, illustrated on page 29, and a counselee located at the right end may seem a disconcertingly huge personal rift.

But the dissonance seems to affect the counselor more than it affects the counselee. It seems that counselees are much less troubled by this dissonance than counselors expect them to be. The counselor's attitude meets a need the counselee feels acutely even if not well articulated.

Of course, a word of transition and definition may be helpful. It can be simple, not elaborate or defensive. The counselor may say, "I find I can be most helpful if I just listen carefully for now." Or, "Before we try to figure all that out, let's give ourselves the luxury of discovering how *you* feel about this." Or, "I think you deserve a chance to figure out just what is happening to *you* in this mess. Let's use our time for that."

Counselees hunger for this attention and support. It becomes a welcome gift.

IN SUMMARY

The counselee feels a personal renewal, literally a newness of self, and a freshness of energy, resources, and strategy. "Born again" even. It's a revival, a conversion of the self from despair to hope, from distrust to faith, from alienation to love.

The counselee arrives saying, in so many words, "I can't cope. I can cope with many things. But something has come up that is beyond me. My usual strategy doesn't work. This is not playing by the usual rules. It's alien. It's a cancerous tumor in my soul; the devil has me. It leaves me helpless, defeated, shriveled. I feel the terror that I am not myself." But pastoral counseling leaves the old self behind. It dispenses a "culture shock" of renewal. It dispenses the "culture shock" of entering into a distinct relationship that is rooted in regard, not in the exchange of affection; the "culture shock" of dealing with problems not by struggling to solve them but by preempting them, by exploring their context and meaning; the "culture shock" of not working with problems but of playing with them; the "culture shock" of the virtual reality, the laboratory of pastoral counseling; the "culture shock" of taking the person more seriously, more substantially, than the problems.

If we find it creditable and meaningful to say, after a two-week vacation, "I feel like a new person," how much more plausible for a person to report after the time-out of pastoral counseling, "I feel like a new person, newly erect, newly equipped, newly robust. My usual method wasn't working for me, but I'm not 'my usual' anymore. I'm ready to try new things." It may be said diffidently, even fearfully—rebirthing is as vulnerable as any birthing—but it is also said with the genuine confidence garnered in the counseling. Stripped naked, perhaps, but glad of it for the promise of new garb.

The Pastoral Counselor
as Witness

The ministry of pastoral counseling is the stringent ministry of witnessing. Fundamentally, the pastoral counselor does not try to "do" anything and is not struggling to make something happen, to make repairs, or to make changes. The intent of pastoral counseling is more profound than that. The pastoral counselor witnesses.

The conversion to which counseling aspires is not a re-vision of tactics, agenda, or will. It is a re-vision of the self. So the counselor's contribution to this is an act of visioning. The counselor does not intervene, strategize, mobilize. The counselor regards, reliably and steadily. The counselor does not condemn, approve, diagnose, explain, or assuage or exert any other leverage over the counselee's life. The counselor witnesses to the fullness of that life. The counselor does not save; the counselor witnesses the saving.

The pastoral counselor witnesses—steadfastly, undistracted, relentlessly—the life experience of the counselee, the harried pilgrimage of a soul that has too often scurried in shadow. Lucid listener, the counselor beholds what has been averted, attests to what has been dismissed, hopes and shames alike. Intervening would be easier and more familiar. Witnessing is a rare and strenuous gift. Intervening would put counselor and counselee in the familiar world of negotiation, the fencing of conditional and guarded trust, the marketplace of affection. Witnessing situates counselor and counselee in a world that transcends the frenzy and the fencing. It calls the bluff of habitual posturing strategies and maneuvers; it renders them meaningless. It says, "What counts is what I see. It counts for being visible and envisionable, not for being good, right, familiar, or easy."

The pastoral counselor's witness testifies to the eschatological hope in which life resides, that alternative reality in which the End of life survives its ending and becomes sovereign, in which meaning prevails over grief, wholeness over dissolution. By demeanor and conviction, more than by word, the pastoral counselor provides a reliable glimpse of a reality as yet unrealized but nonetheless real, in which counselee (and counselor) find a sure niche and blessing. This is the revisioning of life, the *con-version* of life, to which the counselor's witness testifies and invokes.

The counselee may, in timidity and fear, speak of the counseling moment as a haven from the "real world," as though harshness and treachery, hectoring and torment, by default, have the authority to define "reality." But the witness of the counselor testifies that it is just the opposite: reality, finally, is in the completion and assurance savored in the counseling moment; what we, submissively and cynically, dub the "real world" is the distortion. To this eschatological affirmation, the pastoral counselor witnesses.

A TIME SET APART

Pastoral counseling is a time set apart, in a space set apart, in a relationship that is distinctive. It provides a community (usually of two people) that is different from other communities, an alternative world unlike the conventional social world. Priorities are different, customs are different, and the etiquette and expectations of how we treat each other and by which we become a community are different.

The counselor experiences pastoral counseling as a time-out, just as the counselee does. The rhythms, negotiations, and rules of the conventional world are suspended in favor of an alternative world. For both the counselor and counselee, life is moved out of the marketplace into a sanctuary, the pulse of life is converted from the racing irregular tyranny of "if" to a steady "isness." Instead of living an insecure "as if," one can live securely "as is." No less so than the counselee, the counselor is converted from the frantic urgency of being performer, expert, merchant, and consumer to the quiet intensity of being witness. For both, it is a moratorium, a benign suspension of the social contracts and web by which human relationships are conventionally defined and structured. An alternative reality prevails. The fabric of expectations—expectations of what one should give and should get—is suspended and transcended.

For the counselee, this is a gift, often unexpected. For the counselor, it is a voluntary, self-imposed discipline, an ascetic renunciation not unlike the willing adoption of the regimen of a monastery.

For the counselee, the suspension of expectations is commonly more liberating than depriving; the conventional world of expectations has become thwarting and is, for the moment, well shed. The culture shock is welcome, enticing. For the counselor, the suspension is more likely to be a deprivation; the conventional world has provided structure, identity, and satisfactions; so its loss, in the act of counseling, is grieved. The culture shock may be traumatic. Though the counselor's suspension of the rules and roles of the conventional world is a willing choice, it is not always easy to sustain—no more so than any other renunciation and discipline chosen for the sake of religious vocation. As with the discipline accepted, for example, by priests and nuns for their religious vocations, the counselor is renouncing what has been more blessing than curse.

For the period of pastoral counseling, the counselor renounces "the world," a willing sacrifice of its benefits, and invokes an alternative reality so that the counselee can experience relief from the burdens of "the world." Because the social structure has evolved as a tumultuous compromise of many needs and demands, it has ambivalent impact on each of us; it both defines and hobbles, simultaneously supports and saps. In telling us who we are and how to behave, the social structure confers the boon of identity, a repertory of behavior, and more or less assured membership in a community—even as it also constricts and sometimes distorts identity, and dangles membership in a community as a tease. To suspend this conventional social reality for the sake of an alternative is to lose the defining and supporting as well as the crippling. What the counselee needs—and gets—is relief, harbor, and sanctuary. But to invoke this alternative reality, the counselor sacrifices, willingly, the identity-giving support of conventional social reality.

The counseling relationship partakes of the mystical qualities of Martin Buber's I-Thou relationship, a transpersonal encounter in which the usual badges of identity and objectifying tactics of "relationship" are surrendered in favor of what can be called a meeting of pure "beingness."

The counselee is temporarily immunized from the give-and-take negotiations and bartering that maneuver us through life. The counselor renounces those satisfactions and stakes, the succoring and the savoring, that ordinarily energize and direct one's conduct. The stakes are off and the wagering and tortuous maneuvering through conditionalities are over—for the counselee because the connections are temporarily severed between conduct and payoff, for the counselor because he or she is temporarily willing to live without the payoffs.

The discipline accepted by the pastoral counselor is an astonishingly simple one. The counselor is content to be a witness, not a player. The counselor is intensely present to the counselee, but as a witness. The counselor does not crave or design to have an impact, to make a difference, or to leave his or her mark on the counselee's life. Nor does the counselor aspire to find satisfaction, community, or accomplishment. Aspirations that may be perfectly appropriate in everyday conversations—to be curious, to assuage pain, to solve problems, to master perplexities, to understand and know and explain why things are the way they are, to be loved and admired and understood—are put on hold. The pastoral counselor abstains from the normal desire to be included in another's life. The pastoral counselor "gets a life" elsewhere.

AN ASYMMETRICAL CONVERSATION

Pastoral counseling does not have the symmetry and mutuality of conventional conversation. In conventional conversation, both persons have their own distinctive points of view and experiences to offer, and the conversation proceeds by their mutual airing and sharing. Ordinary social conversation is the intertwining of two plots, two story lines. Therein is its fertile richness, in which personhood and relationship thrive, but also therein is the room for mischief, the seedbed in which human distress thrives. In the usual rhythms of conversation we take turns, more or less equally. I listen to your story even while I tell my own (or prepare to). I project and protect my own image/mask/identity even while I acknowledge (or don't) yours. I say, "That reminds me, . . . " "I agree, but . . . " "The way I do (or see, or believe) it is . . . " "No, what I meant was . . . " Every word uttered has two meanings—never identical—one for the speaker, one for the listener. I share the stage: with you, with your perception of me (and/or misperception), and with my (mis)perception of you—there are at least that many of us. The richness and the risks of conversation lie in the interplay of these multiple meanings. It is in such sparring that I forge identity, build bonds, fit you into my life in a way that suits me, and fit into yours in a way that makes sense to you. It is also in such sparring that I may come to feel misfitted, used, abused, twisted, misunderstood, defensive, frustrated, hostile.

But pastoral counseling is one-sided. Counseling provides reprieve and redress from these skirmishes. As counselee, for the time being, I don't share the stage. I have a chance to find out what words and events mean to me, because I can drop my guard against the intrusion of your meanings and against your kidnapping of mine. I can drop my apprehension of your guardedness, my fear that I may upset or misunderstand you. I can drop my obligation to be a custodian of your meanings as well as mine. The counselor renounces his or her social rights to claim or assert meaning, to tell his or her own story, to claim identity. The counselor even renounces the human privilege and need to be defensive; the counselor is willing to let an hour pass, without correcting the counselee's misperceptions of him or her. The counselor replaces the role of player or partner with the role of witness. The counselee replaces the need to engage, accommodate, and skirmish with the enlivening awareness of being closely and unconditionally regarded—a replacement of the mode of "law" with the mode of "grace."

Whatever meaning the counselee's words may have for the pastoral counselor—reminder of similar experiences or troubles, seeming gestures of affection or dislike, challenges to authority or skill, misstatement of facts, misquoting of the pastor, misinterpretation of scripture, egregiously immoral behavior—the pastoral counselor abstains from considering what it means to him or her, and focuses intensely and exclusively on what it means to the counselee.

This distinction is fundamental to pastoral counseling. Here is a crucial test, a common and typical moment in pastoral counseling: Suppose the counselee says, "You don't understand me." A conventional conversation partner is expected and entitled to defend and to smooth: "I do, too, understand. . . . I'm sorry; forgive me . . . Let me try again. . . . " Even perhaps the defensiveness becomes aggressive: "That hurts, why do you have to attack me like that?" But the pastoral counselor puts all these "I's" on hold and witnesses the counselee with a response, perhaps, like this: "That must make you feel lonely again."

Another critical defining moment in all counseling relationships: "Just tell me what to do!" In conventional conversation, that puts the spotlight on the conversation partner, who may yield to the invitation or dodge it ("I don't know what to do either," or, "Let's figure out something together.") The pastoral counselor is content to let the demand linger and to let herself or himself dangle so as to witness to the plight the counselee expresses, maybe with "I guess you feel at your wit's end." The counselor abstains from sharing the spotlight as a player yet, more crucially, assures the counselee that he or she is closely regarded, witnessed.

The counselor is not required to overlook a misstatement or a moral misstep. The point is that if it is reflected ("Actually, you misheard what I said in the sermon." or "You know you crossed a line that time."), such remarks are said in the mode of witnessing the counselee. They are not for the purpose of venting or defending the counselor's views, but for the purpose of inviting the counselee to reflect on the meaning of the error. ("I must have really had X on my mind during the sermon." or "I guess I was just so mad I couldn't stop.")

That is, pastoral counseling does not conspire to cover up or deny misdoing, but probes it. The happy slogan of the 1960s, "I'm OK and you're OK," is *not* the slogan of pastoral counseling. Pastoral counseling wants to transcend the question of "OKness."

Though the counselor is not present to the counselee in the ways of conventional social interaction, the counselor is far from absent or passive. The witnessing is an act of intense energy and focus, astute and attentive. The counselee experiences this moment of focused attention not just as the freedom from social pressures, which it is, but also as a moment of immense support and affirmation, which it also is. The counselor is likely to experience this tremendous investment of energy as exhausting.

THE COUNSELOR'S RENUNCIATIONS

The pastoral counselor abides by a fierce ascetic discipline, relinquishing for the moment of counseling the resources that most bestow esteem and personhood. In the conventional world, status, recognition, and identity are derived primarily from two sources: from relationship, that is, from belonging to another person or group (allegedly the preferred source of female identity), and from successful performance and achievement (the alleged preference of males). But the pastoral counselor renounces both these vehicles of esteem. Pastoral counseling is earnest of an alternative world. Finding personal worth and identity rooted elsewhere, the pastoral counselor does not depend emotionally on either the relationship with the counselee or the successful achievement of any counseling agenda. The pastoral counselor does not need warmth or effectiveness in the counseling, does not court affection or avoid rejection, and does not covet and plot achievement. Such matters are irrelevant to the counselor's self-esteem.

These are monumental acts of ascetic renunciation, essential gifts to the counselee, powerful testimonies to an alternative reality. The counselor's ascetic renunciation is at least as strenuous as that of the monk or nun. For the sake of their religious vocation, monks and nuns surrender—by taking vows of poverty, celibacy, and obedience—the values that the conventional world attaches to wealth and status, sexual intimacy, and autonomy. This is not different from the counselor's vows for the moment of counseling.

The counselor's renunciation is particularly strenuous because, paradoxically, the counselor gives up precisely the resources he or she hopes for the counselee to discover—relationship and accomplishment—or, in Freud's abbreviated statement of the goals of therapy, love and work. Powerful commitments and motivations bring the counselor to the counseling, but if not checked, they will drive the counselor to distort the counseling. If the counselor *needs* the counseling to be successful, *needs* to achieve intense rapport, *needs* to resolve the counselee's distress, *needs* to restore the counselee to abundant life, then the counselor will be driven to forsake the attentive witnessing and to yield to the world's ways of commanding and cajoling.

Four ascetic renunciations can be identified: (1) the expectations of everyday etiquette, (2) the expectations of intimate relationships, (3) the expectations of performance, proficiency, prowess, achievement, and (4) the expectations of clerical or even "pastoral" identity, as this is conventionally regarded. For the sake of embracing the counselee with an alternative set of values and for the sake of steadfast witnessing, the pastoral counselor is ready to be regarded—by the standards of the conventional world—as impolite, impersonal, nonachieving, and nonclerical.

Etiquette

The simple matter of etiquette, the customs and polity by which we all affirm our membership in society, is perhaps more difficult to relinquish than the more intense badges of relationship. Our everyday world is lubricated by social conventions. They smooth the inevitable roughness of human interaction. They keep the peace. They enable us to live our lives with each other efficiently and with decorum without the need to constantly reappraise and renegotiate, without the need to start always from square one. They signal that people are members of the same community, acting more or less from the same script. They attest to the identity and meaning that derive from belonging to a culture, or subculture. They mark the ties that bind people together, even as they also mark the boundaries that divide.

The Pastoral Counselor as Witness

Since pastoral counseling is intended to provide occasion for just the reflective reappraisals that etiquette preempts, a chance to go back to square one, a chance to look under the lid, a reexamination of membership and exclusion that has been taken for granted, pastoral counseling tries to provide a world that is relatively barren of these lubricating conventions.

Here are some of the rules of etiquette that pastoral counseling tries to do without:

Don't let conversation lapse into silence. Always have something to say. Silence may imply disapproval or offense, and such things are better suppressed.

Practice white lies. Questions like "How are you?" "How do you like my new car?" "How was your vacation?" are to be answered with brief positive responses. Conversation is not to be bogged down, nor the mood depressed, with honest, careful responses. (In some subcultures, a deliberately reversed convention prevails; the responses are to be exaggeratedly negative: "It was a vacation from hell; everything went wrong." But this is still a lubricating convention, a cover-up in its own way.)

Reassure distress. Don't let negative feelings or negative news linger without being balanced by a positive remark. "He's better off now." "I'm sure you'll feel better soon." "He's really a good boy."

Show involvement. Perhaps it is more accurate to say "Pretend involvement." Ask questions. Offer advice. Offer to help: baking, driving, phoning. Recall similar experiences of your own. And there's always, "Let's have lunch."

Gather only the facts. Deal with a situation by reciting facts or inquiring about facts. "When did it happen?" "Was she sick long?" "Have you told Jerry?" "We drove 2,700 miles." "The body count was . . . " The purpose, of course, is to preempt the discomfort of expressing feelings.

Explain. Contain distress, distressing events, and distressing feelings by explaining them. "Boys like that do those things." "The cause of the plane crash was . . ." "I could see it coming."

Moralize. This is a form of explanation. Pronounce the difference between right and wrong and explain how any circumstance fits into your firm moral matrix. This is a powerful social lubricant that smooths over the roughness of individual distress. Facts, explanations, and moralisms are a powerful and well-established triad of suppressors of feelings.

The purpose of such etiquette is the socially necessary goal to avoid trouble, to maintain social connections. But the purpose of pastoral counseling is the personally necessary goal to face trouble, to appraise social connections. So pastoral counseling suspends these conventions, at the initiative of the counselor. The set-apart nature of the counseling makes this a relatively safe experiment, and both counselors and counselees report how satisfying and refreshing they find the change. The experience of silence is especially mentioned as a welcome surprise.

But customs and conventions are stubbornly fixed and reinforced, and even experienced counselors are startled to realize how often these forms of etiquette intrude into a counseling world they thought was safely immunized. Counselors usually find that they resort to these conventional responses when they are feeling anxious about some aspect of the counseling.

The Pastoral Counselor as Witness

The difference between the conventional world with its etiquette and the alternative world with its starkness is one of *function*. Each is needed for its own purpose. It will not do to call the conventional world "sick" or "evil." It is not abnormal any more than it is the norm. It is, apparently, as valid and worthwhile a venture at "civilization" as our culture is able to evolve, a social compact that balances by compromise the interests of personal and social welfare, and guarantees the individual a relatively safe niche in the social fabric. But neither will it do to call the conventional world the "real" world. For the alternative world of pastoral counseling is equally real. Indeed, some might claim that it is more "real" insofar as it is, literally, *un*civilized. It affords a glimpse, beyond the life fashioned by the negotiations and compromises of civilizing, of the life as intended by its Creator, as promised by its Redeemer, as guaranteed by its Sustainer. This is life shorn of the need for anxious maneuvers to guarantee one's niche, life blessed by trust, hope, and love.

Ascetic Relationships

Priests and members of many religious orders typically renounce active sexual relationships not because sexuality is deemed "evil," but because their religious vocation requires undistracted focus and because their pastoral role requires immunity from the confusion of even latent sexual relationships. A celibate priest is able to achieve an intimacy with others that is unthreatened and unagitated by even implicit sexuality. The parishioner is able to suspend the usual apprehensions, guardedness, and flirtatious teasing that sexuality provokes because the priest has taken sexuality out of play (insofar as a priest has succeeded in doing so persuasively), and the pastoral relationship can move on to other matters.

The pastoral counselor offers a similar gift to the counselee: the removal from their relationship not just of sexual games and negotiations but of all the games and negotiations that are required to construct "relationships." The counselor is under discipline. The counselor, for the duration of the counseling, is ascetic about a "relationship" with the counselee. Just as the counselor is scrupulous, of course, about separating the counseling from any possible sexual intimacy, the counselor is also scrupulous about separating the counseling from *any* possible "relationship" intimacy.

The priest hears confessions from behind a screen and a psychoanalyst out of sight of the client—symbols of the deliberate impersonality of the event. This is decidedly *not* an occasion for building a "relationship." The two people are partnered in another project. The pastoral counselor maintains the same studied aloofness and nonchalance without the buffer of screen or notepad, but may invent other symbols of the difference, such as a distinctive location, special times, the use of certain chairs just for counseling, or a verbally stated boundary.

"Relationships" are intimate communities (commonly of two people) that nurture, sustain, and delight selfhood; they require constant work, negotiation, and wariness. As with all the ties and constructs of society and civilization, intimate personal relationships are essential to personal well-being; they make us more than we could be otherwise. But, as with all the ties and constructs of society and civilization, intimate personal relationships are also exhausting and eroding of personal well-being; in the compromises they require, they also make us less than we could be without them. The pastoral counselor declares a kind of unilateral disarmament from such habitual jostlings. The give-and-take repertory of "relationship skills" and "relationship building" is suspended because the counselor declines to "give" and renounces "getting."

In entering the counseling relationship, the counselor pledges to abstain from letting the counseling generate a personal relationship with the counselee, in the usual sense of "relationship." Whatever pastoral or personal relationship exists before the counseling emerges unchanged after the counseling. The relationship between counselor and counselee is of an austere disembodied quality, a virtual relationship. The counselor refrains from negotiating any of those mutual satisfactions or mutual dependencies which are the normal part of any healthy social encounter. The counselor pledges not to "need" the counselee, in the usual but complicated way that we, social creatures that we are, normally need each other for a complete sense of selfhood. The counselee is offered a privileged moratorium on just such negotiations and encounters. The counselor abstains from the usual social discourse in which one person finds self-warrant and identity by finding place and regard in the eyes of another. The counselor can provide even and steady regard for the counselee only by renouncing the usual human search for regard from the counselee.

It is an extension of the sexual abstinence. Just as the counselee is offered the privilege of time-out from sexual negotiations or games, so that honest feelings can be risked and energies redirected, so too is the counselee offered the privilege of time-out from *any* negotiations of personal relationship. "What does he think of me? How can I protect or improve his opinion of me? What does she want from me? How can I protect myself from her without losing her regard?" This haunting undertone of all social intercourse is stilled for the counselee by the counselor's renunciation of all such personal claims from the counseling relationship. The counselor does not need the counselee to like or admire him or her, does not need esteem to be warranted or bolstered by exhibiting skills or by any outcome or performance of the counseling, does not have any agenda for the counseling fueled by personal needs.

If the counselee scowls, demands, compliments, complains, behaves aloofly or seductively, such behavior can be viewed for its meaning to the counselee, not for its meaning to the counselor. The counselor abstains from needing it to mean anything. For once, the counselee is spared from having to monitor, censor, second-guess, and ration affect and energy in order to preserve a relationship. There is none at stake.

If the counselee is late for an appointment, or misses one altogether, the counselor refrains from "taking it personally." The counselor has nothing "personal" at stake, has pledged a celibacy of such concerns. So the counselor need not brood on being inconvenienced, demeaned, abandoned—all the affective meaning that such an event might otherwise have for a person. In the pledge of "celibacy," the counselor has renounced any such meaning and is therefore free to attend to the meaning the event has for the counselee.

The counselor's abstinence, like the monk's, testifies to another order of existence; it testifies to a transcending order or world that supersedes the hungers for personal intimacy, which make us lunge and grasp for "relationships" even while leaving us hungry.

The Pastoral Counselor as Witness

Performance and Prowess

"How am I doing?" Ed Koch famously wondered aloud on the streets of New York City throughout his years as mayor. So everyone wonders constantly, often desperately. "How am I doing" in the eyes of others? "How am I doing" in my eyes? In God's eyes? What checklists of accomplishments at the end of a career, at the end of a day, at the end of a pastoral counseling session validate that career, that day, that session? It is a fair, legitimate, and normal question. We should be responsible; we need to be accomplished in measurable ways. It is also a question that drives us to distortion as we try to make the answer come out right. We misperceive and become blind to our failings. Worse, we wrestle the events of our lives to compel outcomes that fit our expectations of success, to create outcomes that readily match our checklists. We maneuver, manipulate, and manage to make others fit our scripts for success.

Pastoral counseling is especially vulnerable to such achievement-driven maneuvering. The counselor is counseling because he or she is called by the most intense and urgent motives to bring others to wholeness and fullness of life. The counselor is afflicted with such high aspirations, such worthy but elusive goals. So the counselor is tempted to manage the counseling and the counselee in ways that yield palpable results, to impose agenda and scripts, to cajole and instruct, to be impatient with hopelessness and doubt, to settle for shortcuts and shallow resolutions, to carry away something that counts as results. The counselor's high hopes become high hoops for the counselee.

But the real intent of pastoral counseling is precisely to spare the counselee just such pressures and hoops and scripts that have badgered and distorted the counselee's life to date. Pastoral counseling provides an alternative world in which the counselee is immune to such pressures.

The counselor renounces the need for the counseling to accomplish anything measurable. It is a huge sacrifice. The counselor is honestly willing to get along without results, to go through a counseling hour, even a year of counseling hours, without knowing whether the counselee's life is bettered, whether the distress is reduced, or whether affirmatives are clarified.

If the counselee expresses satisfaction at results attained or anxiety about results unattained, these are witnessed for what they mean to the counselee, not enfolded into any calculations or assessments the counselor has. If family, friends, or parishioners admire results or fret the absence of apparent "progress," the counselor is not panicked into trafficking with the currency of results. Such remarks can be witnessed and reflected as legitimate expressions of concern ("I can tell you are concerned that things go well") but need not provoke the counselor into abandoning or defending his or her own disciplined approach without the need for results.

The counselor abstains from needing to act wisely, helpfully, or masterfully. If questions are asked, or if there is silence, the counselor doesn't need to have answers or to supply words in order to avoid feeling embarrassed or like a failure. If problems are posed or unsolved, the counselor can leave them that way, unanswered questions and unresolved problems, without feeling it a rebuke or shame. The counselor does not need to garner all the facts before feeling comfortable with a situation; if the counselee's story is confused or incomplete, the counselor doesn't have to be curious or play detective, as most friends would, in order to avoid feeling foolish or out of touch. The counselor has no need to master the perplexities of the counselee's life and of the counseling, no need for a premature closure. The counselor conveys a faith in the validity of the counselee's life and of the counseling process that transcends the conventional but idolatrous reliance on palpable accomplishment.

The Pastoral Role

A minister is often called to give up much of the conventional worldly life, including a comfortable standard of living, privacy for self and family, convenient work hours, clear lines of accountability, immunity from irresponsible gossip and criticism, and adequate staff assistance. But the pain of such surrender is commonly eased by firm vocational identity: "I do it because I am a pastor." And that assertion of identity as "pastor" or "minister" or "clergy" has the content of well-established vocational roles. "I know who I am because I know I am a pastor, and I know I am a pastor because I preach, build church membership, teach the Bible, live a moral and pious life, comfort the afflicted (and—that proverbial symmetry—afflict the comfortable)," and so on through the endless checklist of ministerial skills and tasks. Such clergy roles are badges of identity. To surrender these badges would be an excruciating sacrifice, these hallmarks by which one orders and justifies one's days. Yet that is exactly what a pastoral counselor is called to do for the duration of counseling: to not be a pastor in these conventional senses. The pastoral counselor is not the guide to the moral life or the guide to God, not the expert in prayer or the Bible, not the recruiter to church membership or the leader of worship life. The pastoral counselor enters the counseling naked of the hard-won assurances of what it means to be a pastor (and usually, too, of what it means to be a counselor), stripped of the roles and rules that tell how to assuage distress and chaos.

The pastoral counselor is the agent of that transcendent dimension of life in which such expectations, demands, performances, and checklists, such provings of self, are beside the point. No more than social etiquette, intimacy, or professional success are these vocational dimensions of personhood mean or lesser. For the minister as for anyone else, work and good works are valid and necessary. But they are one-sided, and pastoral counseling represents the other side, the renewing and renewable world of uncalculated, unmeasured, even reckless trust. Pastoral counseling permits the counselor—and hence the counselee—to surrender the dead-end security and indignation of the elder brother and venture the spiritual daring of the prodigal father.

ALICE: CONVERSED WITH OR WITNESSED?

Alice, whom we encountered in the introduction, arrives at your office at the appointed time and says, "I'm really sorry about disappearing last Saturday. I want to make it up. You must have thought I was sleeping in. I only wish I had been."

How does a pastoral counselor respond? If you are a pastoral counselor, or if you want to leave the door open to Alice to pursue pastoral counseling, what do you say that is different from conventional conversation and how do you express it in a way that advances this conversation as pastoral counseling? How do you represent a context that is a benign alternative to the pressing social context that has left her feeling cornered and scrambling?

The key question becomes, in this chapter, Can you disregard any meaning the remarks or situation have for you in order to offer total and unremitting regard for whatever meaning they have for Alice? Can you abdicate all habit and temptation to play a role in Alice's life and become a single-minded witness to her life? Can you perform an act of self-renunciation that would be inappropriate, unwise, and unhealthy in almost any other context or relationship but which is indispensable to those special healing contexts of life that include pastoral counseling? Can you be there entirely for Alice? The moment is all Alice's. Hers is the only agenda; you have none.

This perspective requires a wrenching and rigorous discipline, for there is much in Alice's remark that is provocative, much that seems to invite, even demand your intervention. She assigns you a role as player. There is no stigma in accepting a role as job foreman, or comrade, or a priest hearing confession, or just her harried minister trying to juggle all the needs of the church. These roles just are not pastoral counseling and do not leave the door open to pastoral counseling.

In a conventional social situation, as between friends, or even in a conventional pastoral (but noncounseling) relationship, you would be permitted, even expected, to give voice in some way to your own honest reactions. You are invited to take your part, to hold your own, to be a player, to have some impact on her life.

Here are some responses you might make to Alice, but won't make if you are acting as pastoral counselor.

"The window trim in two of the Sunday school rooms still needs painting." You want to take Alice and her request seriously.

"Sure, we missed you. People were asking about you. You can't 'disappear.'" You want to reassure Alice that she is a cared-

about member of the community, to redress whatever alienation she feels.

"That's OK. We handled things pretty well. Everybody is allowed time off now and then." *You want to reassure and reduce the discomfort of whatever guilt or chagrin she feels.*

"Yeah, it would be good just to relax for a weekend." *You want to express comradely empathy for her seeming desire to sleep in.*

"No, I don't make it my business to accuse you behind your back of goofing off. That's not the kind of minister I am. It never occurred to me that you were just sleeping in." And/or: "I was worried that something was going wrong for you." *You feel misunderstood, miscast as a minister quick to judge, and you want to correct this misunderstanding and to salvage your public image. You see yourself as a caring minister, not judgmental, and you use the occasion to convey this about yourself.*

"I care more about you than about the church getting painted." *You want to explain to her that you have the right priorities.*

"What happened?" *The conventional, neighborly way to be involved sympathetically in another's life—just tell the story, get the facts out.*

"Things can get pretty intense around home on a weekend, I know." *More neighborly probing, maybe even pastoral factfinding—this time with the message that you the pastor understand family disruptions.*

"I sense that you feel a little guilty about this and it still upsets you even after our telephone conversation." *You want to help Alice by providing her with your psychological insights.*

It may begin to seem as though anything you say to Alice will appear on my list as disallowed. That's true, perhaps. We are all trained to be players—participants, actors, contenders, partisans—in the social fabric, and we *want* to be players. We want to like and be liked. We want to help and be helped. We want to have impact on others and to be impacted. These are the ordinary rhythms of human life that are forfeited by the pastoral counselor, because to indulge in them is to forfeit pastoral counseling. It is a wrenching conversion to abandon all the natural ways of relating to Alice that are in your repertory as a human being—or in your repertory as a pastor or counselor.

What is left? How *can* you respond to Alice in the mode of pastoral counseling?

Can you imagine just sweeping your mind clear of all such concerns to fit in with Alice's chronicle, to have impact? To just be a witness, a fly on the wall? The question is not what do you surmise, not what do you think, not what is your opinion, not what should you do, but rather what do you notice. Float. Be empty, effortless, carelessly nonchalant. What do you notice is going on *in Alice*? What do you hear?

She is feeling some kind of distress. Her life is disrupted in some way. Perhaps you may choose other words—*upset, woe, pain, disquiet, disturbed, troubled*. You name it. You know very little about the nature or the cause of that upset. But you do know that her life, at least on Saturday, didn't go the way she wanted. She feels she would have been better off in bed. This is the bald, unadorned substance of what Alice has said about herself. Let her know you witness that.

You don't have to try to do anything more than that. Sometimes beginning counselors think of pastoral counseling as a set of supremely refined skills. It is really much simpler than that. To undertake pastoral counseling is not to pile on norms and expectations of yourself, but to strip them away.

A Gracious Nonchalance

Regarding the Counselee "As Is" and "As Though"

Pastoral counseling provides a safe place for the counselee, an unthreatening, undemanding, unscripted, supportive atmosphere.

Enabled by an ascetic discipline, the counselor requires nothing from the counselee, imposes no agenda.

The counselor conveys an attitude that may be called a gracious nonchalance, a Godly cool. The counselor regards the counselee "as is" and "as though."

This means the counselor does not need the counselee to be different. Regard is not contingent. The counselor does not harbor an idealized picture—as most of us do for each other outside of counseling—of how he or she wants or expects or needs the counselee to be. Most of us traffic in ideals, and we are plagued by the discrepancy between the ideal and the real. We can't help it. Our mind is peopled by the ideal teacher, the ideal minister, the ideal parent, the ideal neighbor, and so on—including, of course, the ideal self—and we impose these ideals as templates against which our real encounters leave us disappointed, disgruntled, and carping. But, having renounced the needs that breed these expectations, the counselor imposes no ideals. The pastoral counselor does not bring to the conversation expectations of the ideal parishioner, the ideal counselee, or even the ideal counselor. However the counselee and counselor find themselves is good enough.

Taking the counselee "as is" does not imply compromise with imperfection. The counselor is not trafficking in discounts and bargains. It implies the absence of any judgment of perfection and imperfection. The counseling encounter is above all that. It disregards discrepancies, the very discrepancies between ideal and real by which the counselee is tyrannized and obsessed. Instead of saying "as is," we can just as easily say the counselor regards the counselee "as though"—as though already the cherished and responsible citizen of the kingdom, a person in mature and faithful relation to God, that the counselee is created and intended to be. The counselor evinces the "as though" regard of God: that the counselee is defined and known not by discrepancy from the ideal, but by the promise of it.

"As is" means that the very "isness," the aseity, of the counselee is what is important, not attributes, contingencies, behaviors, or conduct. It is not a question of whether such things are good or bad, healthy or unhealthy, faithful or unfaithful; the counselee can be expected to arrive at such judgments. It is just that in the regard of the counselor, such questions are not of primary importance. What is of primary importance is what *is*. The counseling conversation is committed to seeing how the counselee *is*.

Of course, the counseling is happening because the counselee is dissatisfied with how he or she is and wants to change. But that is the counselee's judgment, not the counselor's. The paradox is that the counselee is best enabled to make changes by the counselor's disregard of such norms and judgments and by the intense regard of the counselee "as is."

"As is" celebrates what is singular about the counselee. It does not ask how the counselee fits into a class, category, ideal or role. It takes as serious and valid the counselee's distinctiveness, oddness, ambiguities, perplexities, even the counselee's chaos and disorder. Physicists speak of "singularities," free-standing events and conditions that are beyond the pale of the usual laws of physics. One such singularity was the moment of Creation. Perhaps the counselor regards the counselee as in such a moment of singularity, "as is."

The pastoral counselor responds to the counselee's words, deeds, and moods with an evenly hovering attention, indiscriminate, unperturbed, nonchalant, even bland. The counselor does not favor some part of the counselee's account more than others, does not evaluate, does not prefer that the counselee be different in attitude or behavior, does not measure the counselee against standards of psychological health, social responsibility, theological orthodoxy, or ethical probity. The counselor does not read into the counselee's account things that are not said, does not interpret or translate the counselee's story into a psychological or theological language known to the counselor but not to the counselee. The counselor does not diagnose, does not make the counselee fit some previously defined template, category, theory, or label, either of psychology or theology. The counselor does not play detective ("Just give me the facts, and I'll form the conclusion"). The counselor does not try to know counselees better than they know themselves. The counselee's own interpretations get the attention and are not construed as correct or incorrect, but as expressions of how the counselee understands and feels. The counselee is author of his or her own life and is not asked to submit it to the authority of the counselor.

For example, if the counselee expresses exaggerated self-blame, perhaps in connection with the death of a parent or the delinquency of a child, it is not the counselor's role to measure the exaggeration against a norm of "reality" and persuade, cajole, or reassure the counselee to be more "realistic." The counselor does not cross-examine or try to "break" the counselee's account. The counselor witnesses and receives the counselee's account. The intense self-blame is a crucial part of who and how the counselee is at the moment; it cannot be excised without cutting away an important part of the counselee's present identity. This would be to imitate past assaults and invite new distorting defensiveness; counseling is intended to counter such threatening contexts of the past, not imitate them.

The same is true if the counselee is unrealistically blithe about brushing off responsibility, is excessively angry and indignant about a trivial slight, or is passively numb and compliant in the face of abuse and oppression. The counselor notices the irresponsibility, anger, or compliance in a way that makes the counselee curious about it rather than defensive.

The substance of the counseling lies in the discovery of what things mean to the counselee, not in the discovery of what they mean to the counselor.

Because the counselor's "as is" attitude towards the counselee may seem alarmingly irresponsible, let us pause to be clear that the question is not whether such things as guilt, forgiveness, responsibility, reality, self-control, and self-assertion are important, especially in a pastoral ministry. Obviously they are of utmost importance. The goal of counseling is to empower people to live their lives in whole-hearted acknowledgment of just such realities. The question is not of goals, but of timing and of realistic strategy to achieve those goals.

These issues are of such importance that the counselor is careful to follow those disciplines and strategies that best contribute to empowering the counselee to address the issues. This means restraining the natural impulse to shoot from the hip in ways that make the counselor feel better but which actually construct a barrier between the counselee and a new life. The counselee has been admonished, lectured, and scolded often enough in the past, and if such assaultive tactics have left the counselee numbed, blinded, deafened, and crippled emotionally and spiritually, more of the same from the counselor will not help. What will help is the counselor's disciplined, painful suspension of the need for immediate closure, resolution, and remedy in favor of the gracious nonchalance that can accompany the counselees, at their own pace, from their present distorted and partial self-understanding to the fuller openness to life as intended for them.

"MY MOTHER WANTS ME TO COME SEE YOU"

Consider a characteristic encounter. A teenage girl approaches you with the explanation, "My mother wants me to come see you." This is a frustratingly inauspicious opening to pastoral counseling. She is passive, guarded, defensive, uncommitted. So you may well feel like resorting to strategies to structure and focus the conversation, to bring her around to appropriate counselee behavior, to make her admit she has a problem, and to make her want to talk with you about it. You may be tempted to give such responses as, "I wonder why?" "How are things going with you?" "How do you feel about talking to me?" "Let's talk and see how it goes." These are all agenda-driven strategies, agendas of fact-finding, diagnosing, problem-solving, rapport-building. They all reflect some need to manage the conversation, make it productive, or be responsible for it. They all reflect a concern with what the encounter means to you as counselor: a frustration and a challenge.

Or you can abandon such agendas, forsake such need. You can give priority to providing a safe place and simply aspire to witness to what all this means to the counselee. Instead of wondering how you can counsel if she won't talk freely and honestly about her own self, her own feelings, ask yourself how she will learn to talk freely and honestly about her own self, her own feelings, unless you counsel. So you do counsel. You endeavor to make her feel assured and safe, accepted as the perplexed, unfocused, passive adolescent that she is. You witness to her feelings, which seem to swirl in perplexity. So maybe you remark, "But you don't know what you want to say." Perhaps you say something recognizing her as the object or victim of her mother's anxiety. Maybe something like "You're here on assignment" or "So at least we know *she* is troubled" or "She has her ideas about what's good for you" or maybe even "You have to put up with her ideas about what's good for you."

The structuring responses, correcting her and instructing her, evoke continued wary and polite conventionality, a practiced dancing around the issues, and a numbed soggy conversation. "Well, things are going OK, I guess." or "Well, I don't want to waste your time." The counseling response, on the other hand, is likely to brighten the atmosphere and facilitate communication; the presence of the counselor calls the counselee to be present, in some candor and depth: "Yeah, she's on my case a lot" or "I guess she has some reason to be upset" or "You should hear her with my brother."

THE HAPPY CONTAGION
OF NONCHALANCE

The counselor's capacity to accept the counselee "as is"—without a script, an agenda, or an expectation to be different—derives from the counselor's capacity to accept himself or herself in the role of counselor "as is"—without a script, an agenda, or an expectation to be different. It is the counselor's ascetic renunciation of hungers and needs—at least for the moment of counseling—that allows the counselor to be undriven and content about the counselee, to feel an honest "whatever." The counselor feels that neither the self nor the counselee has any need to prove or justify anything; life is assured and justified without need to make it so.

Gracious nonchalance—this unblinking comfort with being the person one is, the dissolving of chagrin and apology for not satisfying some other expectations—becomes contagious. The counselor's nonchalance is tried on by the counselee. Initiated by the counselor into the alternative world, the counselee tries living in it, tries shedding some of the conventional world's habits of covering, dodging, guarding, and begging, and tries regarding his or her own life as it is. Witnessed honestly, the counselee in turn witnesses himself or herself more cleanly, more fully, more spontaneously.

When the counselee feels witnessed and accepted, there is, commonly, a perceptible deepening or thickening of the counselee's account. Something more painful or more perplexing comes to mind. In the long run, this means a gradual evolution from talking about other people and events to talking about self and feelings, an evolution from rehearsing familiar speeches to more spontaneous and unguarded self-discoveries, an evolution from abstract to concrete, from ideas to affect, from judgment to acceptance.

The counselee experiences the counselor as warmly and unwaveringly supportive, as accepting and nonjudgmental, as unconditionally caring, as "all there," as "all for me." This experience is essential, key to the effectiveness of the counseling, necessary to the undoing of the damaging effects of the highly conditioned offers of love to which the counselee has been held hostage in the past, and necessary to the counselee's discovery of being "born again." The counselee must be able to leave behind the bartering for love that has contorted and distorted and be able to venture, in trust, new behaviors and a new persona. The safety of the counseling context permits the counselee to reexamine, undo, and replace those defensive and disabling habits constructed to cope with the threatening and unsafe (or unreliably safe) contexts of the past.

This "as is" attitude of the counselor, this benign context accorded the counselee, is sometimes called "acceptance." Words like *welcome* and *hospitality* also might fit this "come-as-you-are" reception.

PROBLEMS WITH "AS IS" REGARD

Let us consider as directly as possible some of the discomforts a reader may experience in reaction to this chapter and the counseling posture it recommends. The posture of counseling portrayed here may seem too demanding, too permissive, or too mechanical.

A Gracious Nonchalance

Too demanding. Counselors are often dismayed or skeptical about such an understanding of counseling because it seems to impose impossible demands on the personal capacities of the counselor, as though the counselor is expected to muster, out of his or her own resources, a godlike surfeit of gracious love, as though the counselor can supply in relationship to the counselee a constancy of affection that he or she cannot sustain in any other relationship of life, as though the counselor can supply sufficient love to make good all the counselee's scarcity of love. Such a demand, to manufacture and guarantee grace, would be a travesty of high order. Fortunately, counseling does *not* rely on, or require such, superhuman personal capacities of a counselor.

The pastoral counselor does not pretend to possess godlike powers but is a quite humble servant. Quite the opposite of a demand to exaggerate or puff up self, the pastoral counselor is invited to empty self. Quite the opposite of being forced to pretend capacity for an ideal "relationship," the pastoral counselor is invited to renounce "relationship." Quite the opposite of an intense emotional response, the counselor abstains from affect. Quite the opposite of assuming responsibility for guaranteeing benign outcome, the pastoral counselor dramatically affirms the counselee's responsibility by claiming the role only of witness.

The counselor is not an intense presence but a virtual presence, an abstracted presence, a transcendent presence. The paradox of transcendence is that it permits a more fiercely focused regard than is possible from being up close and involved. The pastoral counselor is able to convey an unpolluted regard because he or she is immunized from the poisons that contaminate regard.

Pastoral Counseling

The abstinent counselor, sublimely nonchalant, prodigally detached, cares deeply and unambiguously about the counselee just because he or she doesn't *care*. That is, the pastoral counselor's asceticism wrests apart two meanings of *care*: attending and worrying. The pastoral counselor attends to, loves, and understands just because he or she doesn't worry. The pastoral counselor minds just because he or she doesn't mind.

Too permissive. "Acceptance" sometimes distresses counselors because they feel they are being asked to indulge in permissiveness, to approve or agree with or tolerate certain of the counselee's behaviors or attitudes which they clearly and appropriately disapprove of, disagree with, or find intolerable. But such judgments are not called for. Such counterfeits of acceptance as approval, agreement, sympathy, or toleration are left behind, transcended by the counselor's ascetic self-removal from involvement and investment. The counselor neither approves nor disapproves. The counselor has not the personal investment in the counselee's story that would make such judgments relevant. Counselors are not asked to check their standards of conduct or belief at the door of counseling. Counselors make the much more radical, comprehensive, and preemptive renunciation: they leave at the door of counseling *any* personal investment or involvement. The counselor disregards attributes and doings—all those colorations of personhood that would be and should be of intense importance if the counselor aspired to a relationship or partnership—and focuses, intently, on the sheer being of the counselee, on his or her aseity, on the supremely important fact that he or she *is*, and is the way he or she is.

Too mechanical. But sometimes "merely listening" is disparaged and caricatured as a simple-minded mechanical echoing. In fact, it requires tremendous energy and personal concentration to listen with focus and depth to another human being, especially one who is distraught. The counselor has reason to feel drained and fatigued by a session of pastoral counseling. This investment by the counselor is experienced by the counselee. "The counselor is *all* there for *me*" is what the counselee hears.

The counselor's asceticism is sometimes misunderstood, sometimes even caricatured, as leaving the counselor a cipher, passive, totally withholding of person, of affect, and of presence, an echo-machine. The popular label "nondirective counseling" is misleading because it tells what the counseling is not (which is also important to notice), but not what it is. The counselor is not passive or absent but vigorously active and present, though this presence is not conveyed in the usual give-and-take of conventional social roles, for these are transcended. It is conveyed in intense listening and remembering and noticing. It is conveyed in focused, undivided attention. In stripping self of social attributes and contingencies, the counselor's own aseity, the counselor's own sheer "isness," looms large and thereby invites the counselee's aseity to be acknowledged.

RENUNCIATION AS A CALLING
AND ITS COUNTERFEITS

The pastoral counselor is enabled to prize and regard others by the act of self-renunciation, self-disregard. This dynamic is akin to other instances in which grace and healing become invoked and conveyed by voluntary self-sacrifice. It is precisely the mode, Christians believe, in which God has chosen to restore and to redeem. It suggests the mode of undefensive vulnerability by which followers of Mohandas

Pastoral Counseling

Gandhi and the Reverend Martin Luther King, Jr., have fur-
thered justice and community. It suggests the mode of undefensive vulnerability with which we sometimes are able to
confess our personal wrongdoing and restore a relationship.
Or it suggests the undefensive vulnerability with which we
are sometimes able to accept apology and to forgive.

We all have had a taste of what it is like to find life by
losing it and, more drastically, to find life in another's losing it. We all have had a taste of living by grace.

But we also have had, to our chagrin, a taste of living by
that counterfeit of gracious self-surrender which is in de-
meaning subservience. We have known, and many of us
are still recovering from, experiments, at home or at work,
in which we have been seduced or coerced into surrendering initiative and identity—especially if we are not
among the group of white males whose culture typically
dominates home and workplace. Or we have been seduced and coerced by another's tantrum of deliberate
self-mortification. Especially if we are still recovering from
such experiences, it is painfully difficult to honor a strategy
that seems to call for more of the same in a pastoral counselor's surrender of self. We cringe, quite understandably,
and think "I am still struggling to build or rebuild, to claim
or reclaim a sense of selfhood. Don't expect me to give
away what I have barely acquired or don't have yet."

The difference is that the counterfeit uses an ostenta-
tious self-sacrifice as a weapon or as a tool, as a bargaining
chip in negotiation. The "sacrifice" is conditional. It comes
with an agenda, a claim: I will "lose" myself if you will love
me, obey me, pity me, humble yourself to me. All parties,
especially the "sacrificer," are caught in a web of obligation
and demand, trapped by expectation and need. It is addiction, not a voluntary gift.

A Gracious Nonchalance

The act of self-surrender that conveys grace and renewal is a totally voluntary act, without condition or agenda. The counselor is offering a self-heedlessness. The counselor is not demanding or even expecting anything in response. The counselor's gift does not coerce or restrict the counselee's initiative. Precisely the opposite: it is to liberate the counselee's initiative. The counselor's self-disregard does not diminish the counselee but leaves room for his or her enhancement.

ALICE

Having missed the church cleanup, Alice accounts for her absence.

> I got this weird letter from Dad last Friday that just didn't make any sense, and when I tried to call him that night, he made less sense. So I had to run up there Saturday to see what was going on.

This is intriguing. You are curious; you muse. What mischief is Alice's father into that requires such a drastic response? Maybe a romantic infatuation? You heave an inner sigh of relief that your own father isn't so erratic. Or is Alice overreacting? If you could see the letter, you could tell if it is really so puzzling; maybe Alice is just impatient and impetuous. If the two of you could go over the phone call, maybe you could help Alice's communication with her father. Or maybe Alice was exaggerating the problem with her father because she really was looking for a pretext to get out of the church cleanup chores. But after all, a commitment is a commitment, and the church deserves better than leftover time.

So goes anyone's surmising and pondering, certainly normal for friend and pastor, probing for understanding and for engagement, searching for ways that these circumstances of Alice's life mesh with your own, scouting for ways to fit yourself into her story. You are monitoring, second-guessing, supervising, assessing, diagnosing, judging. That may be a tremendous gift to Alice, reining in her anxiety and anger and marshaling cooler judgment. But it is not the gift of pastoral counseling.

To offer that gift, you accept the discipline and gift of gracious nonchalance. You abandon your legitimate curiosity, your legitimate desire for closure, your legitimate quest for a place in her life. You leave the stage to Alice, and you witness how she is playing the only part that counts. And you testify—out loud to Alice—to what you witness.

If I were the witness, I would testify that Alice is upset and perplexed, that she feels aggrieved and put upon, and that this apparently has to do with her father and the breakdown in communication between them; Alice feels that her father's life has somehow become distorted and is distorting her own. Maybe the words would be something like this: "It must seem like your father's little crazinesses are knocking your own life off balance."

How would you testify? What do you witness?

How will Alice experience such testimony? I think, first, that she will be startled and relieved. She must have worried a bit about the pastor's reaction. Her trip to check with you may resemble her trip to check with her father, and she may have been apprehensive about the possibility of experiencing a similar impasse and confrontation. But whatever she may have been worried about, there is no need. The witness's testimony disclaims any agenda for Alice, any expectations or judgment, any attempt to change her. The pastor is not monitoring or supervising Alice, does not "have a problem" with her attitude, does not grow impatient while she makes a big deal out of something the pastor regards as routine and finished. Neither does the pastor question whether she is taking her church commitments too lightly. She is not "wrong" to have the concerns and priorities and anxieties she has; the pastoral counselor is not in the business of forming these opinions. The pastoral counselor is in the business of noticing her opinions.

The pastor does not challenge her self-understanding. The witnessing takes Alice seriously, does not dismiss or assuage or otherwise treat her feelings (and her) as trivial or inappropriate. It is safe to surmise that anyone else she has discussed this with—her spouse, her neighbor— would have discounted her reactions, made them—and her—feel invalid. They would have had this effect when they avoided the feelings and reverted to ferreting out facts, or when they assuaged them ("It will come out OK") or reproved them ("Why don't you take a drink and relax") or offered in some other way to help her change her feelings. They will imitate Job's friends-turned-inquisitors, unlike God whose response is, "What is, is."

More than this relief, this time-out from deflecting judgment, this moratorium on bartering for place, I think Alice would feel a keen affirmation, a personal validation, an acceptance. "You *do* know how it is. . . . That inner turbulence and churning is not unmentionable . . . it's admissible" will be her feeling. "Yes!" Alice will feel in response to the "Yes!" she hears.

If Alice is seeking counseling, she does not feel that she has a problem as much as she feels that she *is* a problem (as chapter 1 portrayed). What is distressing is not her father's eccentricities but the fact that they bother her. She cannot cope well; she overreacts; she misses a church commitment; she lets her life be disordered. (That she is already judging herself is the most fundamental reason that the pastoral counselor doesn't need to.) Alice's self-judgment, and the judgment of others, is not echoed by the pastoral counselor; but Alice's self-judgments are acknowledged. Alice feels companioned in a way more fundamental and more decisive than any sociable bonhomie. She feels joined and supported as she is, not in a way that demands or rewards that she be something else.

MURRAY

Murray poses a different challenge to the counselor's nonchalance, to the counselor's capacity to accept the counselee as is rather than impose a norm or expectation of how Murray should be different. This also means that Murray demonstrates a special need for the safe place and assurance of the counselor's nonchalance.

As counselor, you have every right to be frustrated with Murray, or at least perplexed by him. He has claimed time after an evening meeting to talk about something which, you must assume, distresses him. But he won't level with you about what upsets him. He talks instead about Sam and Sam's distress.

> I was talking with Sam before the meeting and thought you ought to know what he is going through. Maybe you should talk with him, or maybe find him some volunteer work to do in the church office.

> Well, I think he is finding retirement hard. His heart is still in the office. He asked me tonight if the year-end inventory at the shop was going to go smoothly. You know, he was real proud of the inventory control system he set up. He would go in on Saturdays to keep it fine-tuned.

A Gracious Nonchalance

Well, the whole truth is that now we just scan bar codes in and scan bar codes out, and the computer keeps track of everything that's on the shelves. We just scrapped Sam's system. But I can't remind him of that. It's still his baby.

I don't think Sam was ready for retirement. He doesn't seem to have any hobbies or anything.

You can adopt the strategy, "How can I get Murray to talk about his own feelings and distress?" and you may succeed in requiring or cajoling or inducing some personal account. Or you may adopt the strategy of doing this work yourself, figuring out with clever clinical interpretations the anxieties, for example, that Murray is projecting onto Sam or maybe the guilt he feels about contributing to Sam's plight.

But such strategies, while perhaps satisfying the counselor's needs, contradict the one thing needful for Murray: the safe place that will help him melt the facades of self-assurance and of solicitous care-taking of Sam with which he guards himself, even to the point of sabotaging the personal counseling he (or part of him) wants. Such probing and diagnosis all convey a monitoring and a judgment. It regards Murray as delinquent or deficient. It communicates the opposite of safety and acceptance. It makes him wrap his protective facade all the more tightly around himself.

You have every right to judge that Murray needs to talk about his own feelings more candidly, and you have every right to feel that there is an implicit contract: if you are willing to give him time and attention as a counselor, he must be willing to do the painful work of the counselee—and you have every right to feel misused at the end of a weary day.

Can you give up those rights? Can it be OK with you for Murray to be as he is, mildly defensive and ambivalent about self-disclosure, encoding and enmeshing his own concerns in talk about Sam? Can you take the nonchalant position that this is a perfectly natural and understandable way for a person to behave at some stage of personal discovery and at some stage of counseling? Can it even be OK with you if Murray seems stuck there indefinitely? Can you renounce any *need* for Murray to be articulate about his feelings, any need for the counseling to be "successful," any need to justify your investment of time and energy with a payoff of good work? Does your own sense of self-worth derive from something more stable and more fundamental than getting Murray to follow a script of your preference, as professionally correct as that script may be? Are you sufficiently comfortable with yourself "as is" to be comfortable with Murray "as is"?

The simplest witnessing communicates this to Murray, perhaps a direct remark, such as "It troubles you to have to watch Murray going through this." Or perhaps a less direct remark, such as "It's enough to keep you fretting all evening" or "It seems hard to put that conversation away." Other suggestions appear on page 141.

Empowering
by Tracking Feelings

Alice tells you about her father:

> He's talking about ripping out all the shrubbery around his
> place and putting in sod. At least I think that's what he's talk-
> ing about. He acts like I should know all about it, keeps saying
> I warned him about ticks. But I never heard of any of this.

There are many ways of being helpful to Alice. You can advise on the landscaping, on the pros and cons of shrubbery
versus sod, or on where to get good landscaping advice.
You can advise on how to improve communication between her and her father, or advise her on where she could
get help with the communication problem. She apparently
thinks of her father as a bit demented; you can help her
with this diagnosis and on how to manage the dementia.
You can help her assess her own reaction, to judge whether
she is overreacting. You may have resources to suggest for
the general problem of dealing with aging parents, perhaps a social worker to consult, perhaps a support group
in the church, perhaps a book or a workshop. You can reassure her (for example, "He probably won't do anything
too wild."). You can offer to pray. You can tell her about a
similar experience you had with a parent.

Pastoral Counseling

These are all legitimate ways of being helpful to Alice. When Alice asks for help from people, these are the kinds of help she expects. Perhaps these are also the kinds of help she expects from her pastor. Any of these responses could be deemed, in some sense of the word, "pastoral." But none is pastoral counseling. They all deal with the situation, with the immediate "problem." They help Alice to cope with it. They do for Alice what counseling enables her to do for herself. They apply their help in the coping and functioning realm, the right side of the diagram illustrated in chapter I. They deal with the content of Alice's remarks. They deal with the situation, with norms, with facts, with action and performance.

None is pastoral counseling because pastoral counseling wants to affect Alice, not the situation, to enable her into mobilizing the resources (understanding and insight, responsibility and commitment, self-assurance and self-giving, faith, hope, and love, and more) that will permit her to deal with this and many other situations. Pastoral counseling wants to leave her less dependent on the counselor, not more so. Pastoral counseling is located at the left end of the diagram, in the context domain. Pastoral counseling puts Alice into the central focus, not the circumstances. It deals with what this situation *means* to Alice, how *she* is affected, and how she can affect circumstances. It aims for Alice to know herself comfortably and wholly and to exercise herself coherently.

The best language for such transactions and transformation is the language of affect. Feelings provide accessible vocabulary and vehicle for the soul. It is the witness to feelings that gives access to the inner life, that rescues the self from the hiddenness generally imposed on feelings, and that mobilizes the energies that feelings exert. It is, pastoral counseling supposes, affect that conveys and prospers identity, rather than performance, behavior, or affiliation.

It is by witnessing to feelings that, for most counselees, pastoral counseling enacts the safe place, the environment that allows Alice to drop her guard, to experiment with discovering her own priorities, needs, commitments, resources, and weaknesses. Witnessing her affect admits and validates a disclosure of the self that has been, very likely, closeted in disregard. Pastoral counseling wants to undo what the world has done in communicating the judgment that Alice is unsuitable, because her feelings are unsuitable.

Different counselors emphasize the importance of feelings in counseling for different reasons. Sometimes catharsis, the ventilation and expression of feelings, is thought to be, in itself, therapeutic. Sometimes insight is regarded as the therapeutic key; a person's discovery of the motives and affect driving behavior enables the person to regain control over the behavior. Without denying such benefits, here the recognition and acceptance of feelings is emphasized as the best means for communicating regard and acceptance of the person.

Because the world has commonly used the disparagement of affect as a way to communicate disparagement of the person, pastoral counseling uses witness of affect as the most common means of countering that disparagement.

He's talking about ripping out all the shrubbery around his place and putting in sod. At least I think that's what he's talking about. He acts like I should know all about it, keeps saying I warned him about ticks. But I never heard of any of this.

Pastoral Counseling

The pastoral counselor lets the facts, the situation, the problem wash by and attends instead to the feelings, expressed and implied. The pastoral counselor doesn't try to understand the facts more clearly ("What does your mother think?" "When did this start?" "Where can he get sod this time of year?").

The pastoral counselor tunes into the feelings that are evident, acknowledges them, names them, welcomes them to the conversation. The pastoral counselor identifies consternation, confusion, frustration, annoyance, upset, unstableness. These are the things the pastoral counselor notices and talks about. The pastoral counselor passes over the content of Alice's remarks; instead of her father, she could as easily be talking about a recalcitrant teenager or an arbitrary boss—and maybe will be soon, now that the lode of affect that connects events has been tapped. The pastoral counselor may name the feelings directly ("That's pretty upsetting" or "You must feel quite annoyed") or may imply them ("You don't know what to expect next from him." "What a struggle just to communicate about simple things." "You must feel that you have to be alert, monitoring him all the time." "It makes you wonder 'Who *is* this man?' ").

The pastoral counselor doesn't conjecture or diagnose or probe for meaning and affect not evident. ("Do you often have problems of communicating with men?" "What do you think the struggle with your father is really about?") The pastoral counselor doesn't evaluate or assess feelings ("Are you sure you are not overreacting or picking a fight?" "We have to expect relations with our aging parents to be frustrating.").

In witnessing and reflecting feelings, the pastoral counselor meets Alice where others don't and meets Alice more squarely than others do. The friendly help identified at the outset of this chapter may be important, and it may well be deemed pastoral. But none is helpful or pastoral in the way that pastoral counseling is. None of this helpfulness recognizes Alice as she feels herself. None offers a refreshing, self-reflective time-out from the pressures she feels to be on top of such situations and to make them right, pressures to be a successful performer. All push aside the inner pain and perplexity and torment Alice is feeling (though not saying so) and keep her attention on the external situation. All summon Alice to be strong in her (heroic) posture of coping, managing, surmounting and thereby keeping the worldly pressures on without surcease. All mimic the world's priority on deeds and good deeds. None expresses that most elementary concern of pastoral counseling: "How are you?"

"How *are* you?" "How are *you*?" For someone to care how I feel is a gift. For someone to care enough to listen and really understand how I feel is a greater gift and a rare one. It frees me to be me, a whole me, to acknowledge and embrace parts of myself usually kept closeted because they are usually not welcomed. Feelings are ordinarily a murky part of myself, kept under cover because they are unsettling, even frightening, chaotic. They don't fit well into the neat package I usually present as my self. I disclose my feeling self tentatively and guardedly, even furtively. For someone to witness these feelings matter-of-factly, even whole-heartedly, is to crumble the diffidence and masking.

Being so witnessed helps me better understand and believe the climactic promise of Paul's thirteenth chapter to the Corinthians: "When I became an adult, I put an end to childish ways. For now we see in a mirror, dimly, but then we will see face to face. Now I know only in part; then I will know fully, even as I have been fully known. And now faith, hope, and love abide, these three; and the greatest of these is love."

Feelings are the focus of pastoral counseling for their own sake. This is the substance of pastoral counseling, the arena of meaning and meaninglessness, of growth and its obstruction. Feelings are the focus of pastoral counseling also for an even more crucial reason: because the reflection of feelings, the witness to affect, happens to be a powerful means of communicating acceptance, a means of expressing the unconditional regard for the whole person as is, the no-questions-asked embrace by the prodigal father. It is in the realm of feelings that the counselee—like all of us—has been badgered, belittled, shamed. As particular feelings have been stifled, the self has been stifled and put on guard. As all feelings have been stifled, in favor of the world's preference for fact and deeds, the self has been more thoroughly stifled and put on guard.

In the counselee's history, facts have been used too often as weapons; as means of skewering by agile debaters and cross-examiners; as means of humiliating by relentless teachers; as means of controlling by politicians and media and diagnosticians; as means of humbling one into being a datum, a statistic. "Know the facts!" "Master the facts!" "Stick to the facts!" "Defer to the facts!" have become powerful intimidations. Pastoral counseling disarms these weapons by letting the facts wash by, unmastered and dethroned.

The counselor's matter-of-fact, unperturbed, nonchalant disregard of facts and preference for feelings provide a powerfully restorative sense of self-validity, induce a relaxation of the wary defensiveness that has isolated and beleaguered and stunted. The counselor's nonchalance becomes contagious.

TRACKING THE PARADE OF FEELINGS

Witness to affect works in a sure spiral. Recognition of feelings induces disclosure of more (and perhaps deeper) feelings, which are in turn witnessed, which in turn induces more disclosure of feelings, and so on. If the counselor needs confirmation and reward, this is it. The counselor knows that a reflection of feelings has been on target and effective, not because a counselee explicitly confirms it (although the counselee's response of a delighted "exactly!" is—for all the counselor's disciplined renunciation of the need for satisfaction and achievement—never unwelcome), but because the reflection is followed by further disclosure of affect. The counselee comes to speak of issues that are more and more painful, more and more difficult, closer and closer to the wounds and fears of the inner self.

This spiral of witness and self-discovery shows in the cases of Alice and Murray. Alice moves from annoyance over her father's quirks to deeper angers and sorrows, finally daring to admit her longing for a hug. But this is not likely to happen unless the counselor has accompanied her in earlier, more casual expressions of feeling. Murray comes face to face with his growing fear that his workaholism is based on a false faith, an idol, and so does not deserve and cannot reward the total devotion he has given it.

Murray, as men often are, is less overt in disclosing affect. But his opening remarks leave the counselor with the same choice as in the case of Alice: whether to track the facts or to track the feelings. Does the counselor want to get to know the problem better or get to know Murray better? To solve the problem Murray describes or to provide an opportunity for Murray to grow? To advance in his own spiritual and personal pilgrimage or to come to a conversion of self?

I was talking with Sam before the meeting and thought you ought to know what he is going through. Maybe you should talk with him, or maybe find him some volunteer work to do in the church office.

Well, I think he is finding retirement hard. His heart is still in the office. He asked me tonight if the year-end inventory at the shop was going to go smoothly. You know, he was real proud of the inventory control system he set up. He would go in on Saturdays to keep it fine-tuned.

Well, the whole truth is that now we just scan bar codes in and scan bar codes out, and the computer keeps track of everything that's on the shelves. We just scrapped Sam's system. But I can't remind him of that. It's still his baby.

I don't think Sam was ready for retirement. He doesn't seem to have any hobbies or anything.

As with Alice, and perhaps with most counselees, the initial or "presenting" account seems to be about someone else; someone else is having a problem (Alice's father, Murray's friend Sam). The pastor can be lured into collecting facts and recommending solutions about this other person's problem, perhaps even into intervening himself with the third party. Even if this may be helpful and responsible, it is not pastoral counseling. Visiting Alice's father or Murray's friend would take over the role of your counselee in the relationship, signaling exactly the opposite of the trust and empowering you want pastoral counseling to accomplish.

As with Alice, and perhaps with most counselees, some other pastoral role (you as organizer of cleanup Saturday or you as pastor to Sam or you as dispenser of volunteer church jobs) is used as an occasion or preamble for the conversation. You can fit into this assigned role and become preoccupied with the cleanup or with Sam, but if you do, you should recognize that you are being seduced into avoiding pastoral counseling.

Murray is undoubtedly as ambivalent as most pastoral counselees. We should assume that he wants to lay bare before you some personal concern or trouble, and also that he does not want to. You do him a service in taking the "wanting" seriously and in assuming this is pastoral counseling until proved otherwise. (Chapter 6 will discuss how pastoral counseling embraces the "not wanting.") Pastoral counseling attends to the person at hand, to his feelings, and to whatever sense of distress they represent. The pastoral counselor lets the facts, with which Murray's account is abundantly filled, wash past, and pastoral counseling tunes into Murray's feelings, which are not abundantly explicit, but which are there.

Murray is concerned, uneasy, troubled, upset, or worried enough to hang around after a meeting and talk to you. The pastoral counselor reflects this to him. Certainly, he is concerned about Sam, but that is probably to specify and locate the feelings unduly. Feelings are more general than any particular setting. Feelings have a history and a future, an autonomy. Although Murray's feelings, whatever they turn out to be, may be triggered now by Sam, this is not the first time Murray has experienced them. Nor will it be the last time. That's what makes them important. So the counselor does better to reflect "You are concerned" rather than "You are concerned about Sam" and certainly instead of "You are concerned about Sam not having hobbies."

Pastoral Counseling

Perhaps one of the few rules that can be suggested to pastoral counselors is the Rule of the Subtracted Preposition: use one less preposition than the counselee. Prepositions specify and locate and pin down feelings, whereas counseling wants to loosen feelings and give them freer rein. So if Alice seems to be saying, "I am concerned about my father—about his impetuosity over his landscaping," the counselor's reflection drops the last prepositional phrase. As Alice comes to drop the specific "over his landscaping," the counselor drops one more prepositional phrase "about his impetuosity," and so on as Alice moves closer to her more intimate, urgent, and persistent feelings ("I am concerned . . ."). The same rule applies to Murray's initial string of prepositions, "I am concerned about Sam— over his being without things to do in his retirement." Pastoral counseling will quickly lop off the diverting and specifying prepositional phrases.

The counselor knows that Murray's "concern" has substance and focus that is not yet apparent, but the counselor doesn't need to know what that is in order to recognize the fact of the concern. The counselor doesn't need to conjecture or to inquire whether Murray is seeing his own plight reflected in Sam or projected onto himself, whether Murray is speaking about himself in the code language of speaking about Sam, or whether Murray feels guilty about having contributed to Sam's plight, or whether Murray is upset with the pastor's inattentiveness to personal needs, or whether Murray is reexperiencing with Sam the full-blown Freudian oedipal drama of both delighting and repenting that the pretensions of a father figure have been exploded, or whether the meaning of this episode for Murray is one of the myriad other possibilities that can come to mind. All the counselor needs to know is that there is *some* concern, *some* distress; and all Murray needs to know is that the counselor knows this and is unruffled by it.

LEADING BY A HALF STEP

In the spiraling dance of self-discovery and self-acceptance which characterizes pastoral counseling, who leads? The counselee, of course. The counselor does not tell the counselee how to feel, does not plant feelings for the counselee to discover, does not infer from theory or prior experience what feelings the counselee should have. However, the distinction between leader and follower is not that clear-cut, because the counselee's self-understanding is not that clear-cut. The feelings the counselee discloses are murky, and the counselor can be expected to hear them more clearly than the counselee can hear and express them. That is the skill and gift the counselor brings to the conversation. The counselor *is* tuned, by theory and by prior experience, not to *know* the counselee's feelings before they are expressed, but to *hear* the feelings in what the counselee says with more focus and more precision than the counselee hears them. The counselor is like an archaeologist guiding over terrain that belongs to the counselee but in which the guide can help the counselee to notice things. However, the guide must not overload the archaeological lecture and must not get too far ahead of what the counselee is noticing.

The counselor aspires to stay perhaps a half step ahead of the counselee, recognizing and identifying those feelings that the counselee is just on the verge of recognizing. As good friends sometimes finish each other's sentences, the good counselor may be verbalizing just what the good counselee is about to verbalize. The counselee feels graciously known. If the counselor is too far ahead, the counselee feels pushed, not known. If the counselor is too far behind, the counselee feels dragged back, no more than parroted, not known.

Following the thread of affect is like tracking a path through a maze. Each of the counselee's remarks offers a choice of many paths to take. Some choices will prove to be dead ends, more or less incidental remarks not connected with major themes of affect, or at least not with themes ready to be pursued. Like having a pencil poised at a choice point in a printed maze, the counselor tries to intuit the path that will move ahead and not prove to be a side-track. This intuition is based on several factors. One is a general understanding of what is most important in people's lives (e.g., relationships with major figures, such as parents or the counselor; emotions that are troubling, such as anger or anxiety; emotions that are connected with the self and self-esteem). The counselor's attention is tuned, by study and by experience, to give priority to such signals. Other guidance for the intuition comes from knowing the particular counselee well, discerning the pulses and concerns that energize his or her life. Finally, perhaps intuition is best guided by attending to the wholeness of the counselee's immediate remark. That response is the best response, the one most likely to follow a true path in the maze, which embraces all that the counselee has said—not the response that picks one piece in isolation. Murray says:

> It's a good thing I've got a few years, because I sure don't have time for hobbies now, no time for anything these days. I've got to get home now and polish a prospectus the boss wants on his desk tomorrow morning. Sally's going to be upset when she hears that.

Empowering by Tracking Feelings

A discerning counselor can hear many potentially important themes in such a remark: aging and denial of aging, overworking and harriedness, relations with boss and with Sally, relative priorities of work and family or work and play. But to reflect one of these is to ignore the others and to risk going down a dead-end alley. What is the theme of Murray's remark as a whole? His remark deserves to be taken as *a* statement, not as a checklist of statements. Is there a key word or phrase that seems to illuminate the whole? What do you, the reader, hear?

What I hear—perhaps the most likely path through the maze—is something about Murray feeling his life is distorted, out of control, not what he intends. His life is living him; he is not living his life. Like a runaway truck barreling downhill. "No time for anything" might be the key phrase. "I've got to" seems to capture even more succinctly Murray's mood. Any of these images or phrases might be reflected back to Murray. What I would probably say is a quiet, "*Got* to?" or maybe, "Everything sounds like '*got* to,' " or perhaps, "And you must wonder where *you* are in all this," or, " 'No time for anything,' especially no time for you." I would hope that some such remark would reflect and focus Murray's principal feelings. The purpose is not so much that he acquires the insight of knowing what these feelings are, but that he becomes more at ease with them and with himself.

To present this gift of self to the counselee, the counselor navigates past much tempting and distracting content and deeds—past many lures to be "helpful." The counselor keeps to affect, and steers past much distracting and secondary affect in order to keep to that which most conveys selfhood.

Pastoral Counseling

Alice reports,

> *First thing he said when he saw me drive up last Saturday was, "Did you come on 63 or 117? You know it's three miles shorter on 117." I can never get him to realize that 117 goes through the center of two towns, with all that traffic. I should know—I've had to make that trip enough.*

We sidestep the content and discern, What is the gist of affect she conveys? To discern this, we listen to her remark, to the whole of it, as best we can; we also know Alice as an individual person as best we can; and we also know Alice as a characteristic human being, as best we have learned about human nature.

The loaded words—the three times she says "I"—are "I can never get him to realize," "I should know," and "I've had to . . ." We bypass the predicates that specify content, so as to "liberate" the feelings from the particular arguments and choices and chores that have triggered them. There is annoyance and irritation present, anger, belligerence, competitiveness. But we know, from acquaintance with Alice, that such belligerence is unusual; it has a focus here, a particular reason for being here and now. And we also know, from study and experience, that such anger does not appear in a vacuum. Anger is often a way of saying "Ouch." Can we hear in Alice's remark any of the larger affective context, any of the "Ouch," any of the anger's immediate reason for being, any of the frustration or disappointment that has provoked it? If not, we wait until we do. If so, we witness to what we hear.

The loaded words, it so happens, run together into sentences and spell out the larger affect: "I can never get him to realize that I know . . . I can never get him to realize that I've had to . . . I can't get him to respect what I know and do. I can't get him to appreciate me . . . " This reading of her words checks out with what we know about Alice, who has been so scrupulous and energetic to get her minister's OK about her absence from cleanup day. It checks out with what we know is often the case between fathers and daughters. It checks out with her emphasis that his reproof of her was his only greeting. So the counselor finds words to reflect this package of affect. Perhaps, "Some greeting," or maybe, "How annoying not to be appreciated," or maybe something in between.

"YOU SOUND ANGRY"

Anger is worth special attention as we explore the delicate art of reflecting feelings. A counselor might be inclined to respond to Alice, "You sound angry." Such a response appears often in pastoral counseling conversations, but more often with beginning counselors than with more experienced counselors. Anger is an intense affect and one generally suppressed, so the beginning counselor supposes that to name it, and to accept it is an important step in counseling. That may sometimes be the case.

But it is also often the case that to name the anger out of the context of frustration and disappointment that has provoked it is so incomplete that it becomes confrontational. If the affective nexus from which the anger is derived is not also acknowledged (affective nexus, not factual situation), it is very hard for "You sound angry" not to be heard as "You sound angry without cause." There is a good chance that the counselee may interpret it as an accusation. If there were a long-term counseling relationship and commitment to rely on, then it might be useful and therapeutic to examine the counselee's readiness to feel accused when the counselor makes an essentially nonjudgmental observation. But in beginning and short-term counseling, providing the safe place has the highest priority, and whatever threatens that, whether reasonable or not, needs to be avoided.

"You sound angry," without acknowledging, too, the context that provokes the anger, has another drawback. It may sound mechanical, glib, a caricature of counseling. For all the intensity that anger possesses, and despite the fact that it is often buried, to name it by itself may seem superficial, obvious. The counselee may well think, "Of course I'm angry, but I wish you could hear me more deeply than that."

THE AWKWARDNESS OF REFLECTING FEELINGS

The beginning pastoral counselor is likely to feel at least four kinds of discomfort with this chapter—that is, with the view that reflecting feelings is the principal strategy of counseling. One is the overarching concern that this is not *pastoral* counseling, not ministry, not religious. This concern is crucial and deserves a chapter of its own, the last chapter. There are three other issues that will be discussed more briefly here. All express an awkwardness a counselor may feel. All represent, I think, the lingering taboo that attaches to feelings and their expression.

(1) "It feels artificial," counselors sometimes say. It is not normal conversation. It is chilling, heartless. It is, paradoxically, intellectualizing because it is talking *about* feelings. It is a kind of private trick by which the counselor dodges real participation in another's life. It objectifies what is ineffably subjective.

To this, I think, there are two simple suggestions. One is the reminder that the purpose of pastoral counseling is to be "different," not "normal" or usual. The artificiality is intended by the counselor's ascetic renunciation. The counselor isn't supposed to feel sociable, "in relationship." The other response is to say simply, "Try it." Experience almost always reassures. Witnessing to feelings does bring a connection, even though not the customary social relationship, and summons a richness of encounter. People's hunger for such witnessing overrides—for the counselee if not always for the counselor—whatever artificiality or awkwardness there may be in the limits of the exchange.

(2) "It seems trivializing, privatizing." The strategy of reflecting feelings seems artificial in another sense. In slighting what has here been called the situation, the facts and conditions of a person's life, in favor of internal feelings, pastoral counseling may be bypassing the most urgent needs of counselees. People are often contending with abuse, injustice, inadequate access to power over their own lives, as well as with hunger, poverty, illness, and death. These things cannot be modified by a counselor's reflection of the over-powering feelings they induce, and the feelings are not likely to change until the circumstances change.

There are two responses, I think. First, this *is* a limitation, a serious limitation, of pastoral counseling, not of a particular strategy or style of pastoral counseling. People do need and deserve assistance and ministry beyond what is available from pastoral counseling. But, second, pastoral counseling can make an essential contribution insofar as it can empower people to deal more adequately with the situational distress. Pastoral counseling, for example, can help mitigate the *self*-abuse that abusive situations induce and that inhibits dealing with them. It is when situations are most desperate and damaging, I believe, that it is time for the best pastoral counseling, not time for compromising the counseling.

(3) "I can't hear the feelings that clearly. I must be tone-deaf to affect." Discerning the affect in remarks by Alice and Murray can be daunting if it seems to demand a facility one doesn't have. "How can you read all that into (or out of) a sentence or two?" is a legitimate question.

Again, two responses, both personal: first, this incongruity or disparity is inherent in a book as a form of communication. As writer, or so I believe, I am supposed to display more thorough reflection than I could possibly display on the spot in the midst of counseling. The purpose, or so I believe, is to prepare me and you to be somewhat more sensitive the next time we *are* on the spot in the midst of counseling. It's regrettable if it also has the effect of intimidating, or of encouraging either of us to take undue refuge in books. Second, I have observed that counselors—myself included—are much more comfortable and fluent in identifying affect *after* a counseling session than in the midst of it. In reviewing a session, counselors are much more likely to comfortably identify feelings than they were in talking with the counselee. This suggests two further observations:

First, it is important to recognize the lingering power of the taboo, which still besets us all as counselors, against disclosing or discussing personal feelings with each other. What makes it so important to do makes it hard to do.

Second, it is vitally important to develop and maintain fluency with affect by regularly reviewing counseling sessions, in detail, with a mentor or supervisor, or with colleagues, or by yourself. How many hours do you commit to preparing a twenty-minute sermon? Pastoral counseling also demands behind-the-scenes preparation—perhaps a three-for-one time commitment (for each hour of pastoral counseling, two additional hours of reflection). If you don't have that much time available, your answer to the question, "Do you have time to talk with me?" may have to be a regretful, "No." Spend one hour immediately after the counseling recalling what happened. Jot down the gist of exchanges. The recollection of the rhythms of the conversation helps to keep your listening acutely tuned and provides you with a record from which you can learn by going through the event a second and third time. Spend another hour reviewing the conversation with a colleague or mentor, preferably someone with whom you have no other relationship, certainly not a spouse or member of your church or church staff, and certainly someone you can totally trust to keep the conversations confidential.

Ambivalence,
Resistance, and Re-covery

The foremost rhythm of counseling is that of unwrapping: In the uniquely safe place that counseling provides, the counselee discovers and welcomes into his or her life feelings and memories that have been covered and unwelcome. We often take for granted that counseling is defined by this process of uncovering, and we suppose that if this unwrapping is stymied, counseling is not doing what it should. Most discussion of counseling—this book being no exception—tends to identify effective counseling with the discovery and disclosure of buried feelings.

But in fact, though such unwrapping usually happens, it does not always happen. It doesn't have to happen. The preceding chapter portrayed the language of affect as a *means* of counseling, not the goal. Affect provides one vocabulary by which understanding and acceptance can be expressed. The counselor accepts feelings, does not demand them. Unwrapping does not define counseling; witnessing does.

There is a counter-rhythm that belongs to counseling as much as the unwrapping. That is the rhythm of wrapping. It belongs to counseling because it belongs to normal human experience. It is a mature and healthy part of the self that on appropriate occasions finds it necessary to contain or ration affect. It is inevitable and ultimately useful that the counselee sometimes abandons the process of discovery and, instead, comes to restrict feelings and memories. This re-covering is part of the process of recovering.

To put it slightly differently, the affect to which the counselor provides attentive, reflective witness can include a kind of nonaffect or antiaffect. Numbness, dumbness, and silence are as valid as outbursts of rage or tremors of anxiety.

Ambivalence—feeling both ways—is an inevitable and appropriate attitude towards the important persons and the important affect discussed in counseling, and therefore towards the counseling itself. Just as the counselee feels a blend of positive and negative feelings towards parents, spouses, and others, and just as the counselee needs both to pour out and to control strong feelings, so too the counselee both welcomes and resists the counseling itself, its special sanctuary and safety, its discoveries and unwrapping, its special attention to those areas of life that are the most complex and troubled and therefore most fraught with ambivalence. So the counselee may turn silent, or silent about important issues, may turn aside to gossipy or trivial chatting, may forget an appointment, or may find any one of innumerable other ways to suspend or even subvert the work of the counseling.

The traditional term for this process, following Freud's usage, is *resistance*. If this term seems to convey a scolding or blaming, as though the counselee is out of bounds or inappropriate, then it may be better to use the more purely descriptive phrase "ambivalence towards the counseling."

Ambivalence, Resistance, and Re-covery

This chapter will use both *resistance* and *ambivalence*, understanding both as merely describing those moments when the counselee is calling time-out from the process of unwrapping and engaging in containment.

It is quite understandable that the counselor may be tempted to experience this ambivalence as disruptive, even hostile, as obstructing the movement of counseling, as violating the partnership. The counselor may well feel stranded, abandoned. "How can I reflect feelings if you are not expressing any? How can I accept if you disclose nothing problematic to accept? How can I be a counselor if you will not be a counselee?" the counselor may protest silently (or not always so silently). Insofar as the counseling is tied to the unwrapping, it is stymied. The counselee's tactic seems to require the counselor to forsake the counseling role and revert to precounseling management, to undertake emergency action to jumpstart the counseling. The eminent counselor Carl Rogers regarded such covering behavior as the symptom of flawed counseling.

This chapter will demonstrate that the resistance is not the obstruction of affect-expression and self-disclosure but is, rather, another form of revealing and embracing feelings and character. It does not end the counseling conversation; it provides another topic for that conversation, an important topic because it is a situation immediately at hand. The resistance is not a threat to the counseling, not an emergency, not a symptom that things are going badly but a sign that things are going normally. The counselor need not panic or "take it personally," or abandon the steadily attentive attitude. The counselor's response to resistance is the same as the response to any other expression of the counselee: to witness it.

WHAT DOES RESISTANCE LOOK LIKE?

Consider Alice's question to you, "Well, which road would you take?" She has been delving, with increasing feeling, into her troubled relation with her aging father. She has just touched on some irritation at having to make frequent visits, which the father acknowledges not with appreciation but with badgering about her driving. You have heard, understood, witnessed, and accepted her burgeoning annoyance and disappointment.

But she abruptly turns aside from this encounter with her father and asks you about your choice of driving routes, "Well, which road would you take?" For the counselor, this can be a perplexing, frustrating, and annoying moment. Counseling that was going smoothly and getting gradually deeper seems to have unilaterally stopped. You are out on a limb. You are deprived of your role as counselor because Alice seems to have suspended counseling, and you are forced into the role of referee or travel expert. Or so it may seem. The purpose of this chapter is to suggest that the counseling is continuing, to change the logical non sequitur into a psychological sequitur, to change the "But" that began this paragraph into a "So."

Murray, too, suddenly stops talking about his dilemmas with Sam, with Sally, and with work and talks about you: "You're lucky not to be in this rat race." How disconcerting to have Murray halt his gradual self-discoveries, especially when he has just begun to touch on the task hanging over his head this very evening and on an unpleasant confrontation with Sally, which is about to happen. How doubly disconcerting to have Murray inaccurately describe your life as exempt from the "rat race," as though you can't genuinely appreciate his plight. It must be tempting to be totally lured out of the counseling role, to educate Murray on your work life, and to display your credentials as one who does know what it is like to feel oppressed by work demands.

Resistance takes many forms: the counselee forgets to keep an appointment or forgets a crucial insight achieved earlier; looks blank when the counselor refers to things the counselee has talked about earlier; makes flippant wise-cracks; consistently misunderstands the counselor; falls totally silent; chatters unreflectively about inconsequential matters or about people far removed; demands the counselor's opinion or advice; picks a fight with the counselor; muses or debates abstractly about theological or psychological or economic theories; launches a fact-filled chronicle of some recent event, without suggesting any emotional nuances; frets endlessly and with confusion over scheduling another appointment ("Well, Tuesday is probably OK for me, if they don't call a meeting, unless Wednesday is really better for you"). The counselee may announce that there wasn't really a problem after all, or that it is all solved. These forms of resistance can go on and on as the counselee relentlessly wraps things under highly protective cover. The counselor may well feel outsmarted by a resourceful adversary, may feel the counseling subverted.

However, it is more accurate to regard these expressions of ambivalence—even, or especially, when they seem targeted at the counseling itself—as constructive components of the counseling, not as merely obstructive. In the resistance, the counselee is bringing to the arena of the counseling another facet of his or her emotional life, a crucial facet.

The counselee comes earnestly craving to grow in intimacy or in self-confidence—and just as earnestly (though perhaps less consciously) fearing intimacy or avoiding self-assertion. The counselee yearns to know and reveal himself or herself more wholly—and dreads it. The counselee longs to change—and also clings desperately to those familiar patterns that have evolved and become established just because they suit. The vexing and troubling issues that bring a person to counseling are the very issues most loaded with ambivalence, which is readily transferred to the counseling process itself.

So the counselee who especially needs counseling, who wants counseling, who works hard and with commitment to the process, is also a person who needs to find ways to resist and sabotage the counseling.

If the resistance is reprimanded or engineered away, then some part of the counselee is denied access and the counseling is attenuated. What the counselee experiences is the message that such ambivalence is unacceptable. Some part of how the counselee "is" is not acceptable "as is." The counselee learns that the pastoral counseling is *not* different from the daily world, that affection is to be bartered for, that the counselor's unwavering witness wavers, that the counselor can be manipulated.

THE TEMPTATION TO PERSONALIZE
THE AMBIVALENCE

A counselee's ambivalence, expressed as resistance to the counseling, poses with excruciating sharpness the counselor's choice as to whether to regard the events of counseling for what they mean to the counselee or for what they mean to the counselor.

The temptation for the counselor to take the ambivalence personally is unusually strong. The counselor may easily feel abandoned and betrayed. For by the time the resistance is mobilized, the counselor and counselee are likely to have formed a firm partnership. The counselor may well have been effective in fashioning an accepting and safe environment. The counselee may well have responded with courageous candor and self-discovery—unwrapping. The counselor maintains his or her part of the teamwork, when suddenly, without warning and without visible reason, the counselee abandons the team.

If this were a usual personal relationship, the resistance would reflect a souring of that relationship. Things that were going well and intimately between two people have gone wrong. One or both people feel wronged ("How can you do this to me?" "What did I do?"). It would be time to stop and repair the relationship, to work through the rupture, to express disappointment and hurt, to assign responsibility, to accept blame. These are normal and healthy responses to a disrupted relationship. And this is what counselors are tempted to do when they regard the counseling partnership as a relationship, when they have not entered the counseling with an ascetic renunciation.

Counselors are sometimes ready to blame themselves. They suppose the resistance follows from their own failure to afford a sufficiently safe and comfortable atmosphere. "What did I say that was too threatening or rejecting?" is the frequent self-scrutiny, and the answer often is, "I interpreted too deeply and too soon" or "I failed to understand." It is true that counselors sometimes do overinterpret or otherwise fail to be steady accepting witnesses. But the presence of resistance by itself is not sufficient evidence for this, since the ambivalence is already brought to the counseling, as to all situations, by the counselee.

Pastoral Counseling

Counselors are sometimes ready, implicitly or explicitly, to blame the counselee, to accuse the counselee of breaking down the counseling process. The counselor, in response, also abandons the counseling and resorts to administrative or educational or exhorting modes. The counselor instructs, scolds, or coaxes the counselee to stay with the unwrapping—thereby rejecting that part of the counselee that needs, for now, to rewrap. The counselor practices damage control, engineering, managing. In the mood of emergency, the counselor resorts to noncounseling tactics to jump-start the counseling. Ironically, the clear message is: we can rely on the methods of counseling to solve "your problem," with your spouse, for example, but not "our problem" here and now; for that we must resort to old-fashioned exhortation and management.

Sometimes the counselor's blaming takes a form that often appears in "relationships." Psychological insight is used as a weapon. "That's your baggage," the counselor accuses. "You are playing old tapes. You are treating me the way you (want to) treat your mother." And you shouldn't do this to me is the implication of the scolding; I don't deserve it. Well, such insight may be accurate, but in counseling this is a matter for disinterested witnessing, not scolding. The counselor who has parked ego at the door can muse helpfully but not insistently on how "maybe we can see right here what happens between you and your mother."

This blaming approach assumes there is something wrong, a flaw, a defect, a delinquency. This book assumes that the ambivalence and the resistance it generates are part of the Creation, not part of the Fall, not anyone's sin. The ambivalence and its expressions are part of the way people are and the way they are supposed to be. Ambiva-

lence is a healthy and adaptive disposition, just as re-
pression is an essential skill and defense mechanisms are
fundamental components of healthy character. Without
these skills of control and self-rationing of affect, we would
be too vulnerable to survive.

This blaming approach puts counseling in thrall to a
work ethic, a goal-driven need to repair, remedy, fix, an
abandonment of the counselor's stance of amazed, spell-
bound, transfixed witness to what is.

This blaming approach and the frustration that generates it assume that the resistance is an abandonment of
the realm of affect. They fail to recognize that the resistance represents intense emotional engagement. We now
turn to a closer look at what that intense emotional engagement may be.

WHAT DOES RESISTANCE MEAN
TO THE COUNSELEE?

If the counselor can maintain discipline, renounce a personal stake, and listen for what it means to the counselee,
this sudden lurch from unwrapping to wrapping, then it may
seem a relatively routine part of the counseling process to
hear, understand, accept, and reflect the ambivalence.

The counselee *is* expressing feelings, the powerful
counter-feelings of avoidance. The counselor with ears to
hear will perceive this ambivalence as clearly and as
calmly as any anger or guilt or yearning. Feeling stunned
or numbed or apprehensive (by a surfeit of unfamiliar and
uncomfortable feelings) *is* a feeling. The counselor who is
committed to understanding, accepting, and reflecting a
counselee's feelings—whatever they are, without regard
to any preferences or expectations of the counselor—will

find ways to understand, accept, reflect *these* feelings of ambivalence.

It should hardly be surprising that the human personality, indeed the human soul, is characterized by matched polarities. The universe is so structured. Stars and galaxies are spun into movement and held in place by the matching centripetal and centrifugal forces of gravity and orbiting, by titanic duels of implosion and explosion. Atoms are structured by the matched polarities of positive and negative charges simultaneously challenging and charging each other. Organisms are made alive by the throbbing balance of enzymes that trigger and contain each other, by the rhythms of breathing in and out, mimicking the tides that first nourished life. Animals are sustained in motion by the rhythmic flexing and extending of muscles. We most trust our governance to the checks and balances of competing factions, and our economic welfare to the delicate dialectic of supply and demand. Why not expect the emotional life to be similarly animated by balanced polarities. It is.

Our deepest longings are locked together with our deepest fears, our strongest likes readily unravel into strong dislikes. The same persons and situations to which we are most fiercely attracted and attached can trigger astounding antagonism and aversion. Logical contradictions are lodged in our minds as psychological partners, so that if I ask you what comes first to your mind when I say "fast" you say "slow"; so it is with hot and cold, up and down, in and out, love and hate. Our lives are constructed—not distorted, as it sometimes feels—by ambivalence, by double messages we give ourselves and others.

What do you hear when Alice says, "Well, which road would you take?" We know what this means to the counselor—if the counselor lets it have personal meaning. It is putting the counselor on the spot, misunderstanding the role of counselor, making the counselor a referee or a travel guide or a casual conversationalist. What does it mean to Alice? What do you hear?

At the very least, it is some kind of bid for a time-out. Alice might have said, "Let's get back to the church cleanup tasks." or, "By the way, have you noticed there is a new shopping center being built on route 63?" What the counselor experiences as abandonment of the searching and unwrapping is exactly that. However, this is not regarded as a flaw or problem but simply as a fact—an interesting fact. Your response can reflect this interest, without censure or rebuke: "I guess it feels like enough about you and your father for a while; you want to hear from me," or, "Road maps *are* easier to talk about than fathers."

The apparent feelings are those of avoidance. Alice has just expressed annoyance with her father. Now she shows us that she is apparently accustomed to wrapping this annoyance in avoidance. The counselor witnesses to the avoidance, calls it to her attention, accepts it. As we expect any witnessing of affect to spiral into more expression of affect, once the avoidance is witnessed to, we may expect Alice to show more intense feelings of some kind. Her avoidance attended to, Alice may respond with an intensification of the avoidance; for example, she may express despair over the seeming futility of talking about her father. ("What's the use. Thanks for your time.") Or, as did happen, she peers and peels below the avoidance and finds deeper annoyance and anger at her father. Witnessing to her ambivalence has brought it to the surface and accepted it as the immediate problem for her to work on. And she has.

"Well, which road would you take?" Perhaps you hear not only the avoidance but the pain that prompts it, and you witness this: "This thing with your father is too painful to talk about very long," or "If only there were a road map for dealing with fathers!" or "This battle may seem so painful, you'd like a referee just to settle it," or, "It must feel like this conversation is getting a little too hot to handle. Need some time to cool it?" or, "It seems like seeing your father in this new way is a kind of a shock, like an electric shock, and you have to let go of that wire and put some protective gloves on."

In Alice's question, perhaps you hear more than avoidance and plea for a time-out, and the pain that prompts it. "Well, which road would you take?" Perhaps it is a bid for an ally in the battle with her father over which of them is the competent one. Her question may translate as recruitment into her lifelong battle, "Do you agree that I know what I'm doing and he doesn't?" What the counselor may be tempted to resent as a seduction out of the nonpartisan role of counselor into assignment as referee or ally is exactly that. But there is no need to resent it, just witness it. "Looking for an ally?" or "Do I think you know what you are doing?"

Perhaps it is more than the role of ally you feel recruited to. Especially as you reflect on Alice's insistence on apologizing for missing the cleanup day, you, who only want to be a counselor, perhaps feel recruited into being the good parent. You are aware, nonjudgmentally, of the irony that she seems dependent on you to certify her independence and competence. You *might* reflect this to Alice: "You would trust my opinion more than his?" or "My approval might help make up for his disapproval?" or, "It's awfully hard to be as independent and confident as you would like.

Such reflections of resistance become reflections of attitudes and feelings that are here and now, immediately present in the counseling encounter, incarnations of attitudes and feelings that are important in all crucial life situations.

Murray, too, exhibits this resistance. Just as he seems to be digging more deeply into his self-awareness, he abruptly breaks off and turns to you, "You're lucky not to be in this rat race." Bypassing all the defensive and corrective protest that would be induced by the counselor taking this personally, what does the remark mean to Murray? What do you hear? What is the affect in this remark?

At the very least, it is a change of focus, a disruption, a time-out. But it does not occur at random or in a vacuum. As abrupt a change as it is, it is not discontinuous with what Murray has been talking about, but directly and immediately continuous with it. The glibness and superficiality of Murray's remark does not mean that the counseling is not digging deeply; it means that it *is*. If you need confirmation that Murray's take-home work and his relation with Sally—the matters he has just been discussing—are emotionally important to him, this resistive statement to you provides that confirmation. The thrust of avoidance is to counter some troubling affect that has been conjured up. We can surmise—and reflect—that much without knowing precisely *what* the provoking affect is.

If you respond with something like "When you're in deep water, you need to come up for air sometimes," it may seem a logical non sequitur, unresponsive to Murray's remarks about Sam, about his own life, or about you. But it makes perfect sense psychologically as a response to what Murray seems to be feeling in this conversation and in the life that this conversation is about. You may be surprised how welcome is the disregard of the literal question in favor of the sensitive regard for its feeling content. Or perhaps simply and directly, "I guess it's easier to talk about me than your boss or Sally," or, "Thinking about Sally's reaction makes you want to change the subject."

Maybe you hear not just pain to avoid but more of a longing: "I guess you'd like to think there is a possibility of staying out of the rat race." Or, "Misery loves company, and you'd like to have some."

In the actual conversation, the counselor's acceptance of the resistive statement and the feelings behind it has yielded a remarkable deepening by Murray, who responds to the counselor's honesty by looking honestly inside his own emotional life for the first time in this conversation and finding there a workaholic; the burden of work is not just imposed by others but is his own addiction. You might say Murray was enabled to deepen by having his shallowing accepted. The resistance proved to be a crucial turning point in Murray's counseling.

Getting Started
Precounseling or Counseling?

Pastoral counseling evokes an alien reality. That is what makes it effective. That is also what makes it difficult to en-act. It is a reality in which the pastor is not an authority (in any worldly sense), not a judge, not even a participant, but a witness. It is a reality in which a person may trust rather than maneuver, in which a person speaks freely, not guard-edly, in which a person speaks out of inner promptings, not by the promptings of others. It is a reality in which one comes to trust friendly powers more than hostile powers.

How to make this transition can be a formidable prob-lem for both counselor and counselee. The culture shock of entering the counseling reality is especially abrupt and disconcerting for the counselee because it is so new. The alien reality which is the world of counseling may be re-freshing and welcome, but it is still alien. If the time-out of a vacation often takes a person days to get used to, still more does the time-out of counseling.

This chapter raises the question whether the transition is to be viewed as preliminary and prerequisite to counseling or as part of counseling. Does the counselor postpone being a counselor until the counselee is "ready" to be a counselee? Does the counselor postpone the role of witness and instead explain, instruct, coach, and manage? Before being a counselor, does the pastor have to be teacher of the rules and roles of pastoral counseling? Does setting up a counseling session seem to a pastor analogous to recruiting and training Sunday school teachers or arranging a committee meeting? That is, is administering the prelude to ministering? Is it like setting a stage for a play, like working hard to arrange a vacation to relax in? Like teaching rules and strategies before playing the game? Like dealing with the tension and the maneuvers and the "best behavior" of courting in anticipation of establishing a home to relax and "be oneself" in?

PERCEIVING "AS THOUGH"

This chapter proposes that the transition is definitely part of the counseling. The counselor witnesses the distress and struggle of the transition as the counselor would witness any other distress and struggle. The counselor does not try to salve, solve, bypass, or remedy the distress and struggle of the transition any more than he or she would any other distress or struggle. What the counselee learns from the transition—such as learning to trust and learning to listen to oneself—are privileges too important for the counselor to dare to usurp.

Whatever "content" or "problem" the counseling addresses, the most important benefits—what make pastoral counseling pastoral—have to do with just the stress of transition, the stress of learning to live in a safe world, the stress and the joy of living in the kingdom "as is," of living in the world "as though" in the kingdom. The counselor contributes to this discovery by regarding the counseling, from the beginning, "as though" it already were counseling. And such regarding makes it so.

Getting Started

The pastoral counselor witnesses, as though it were counseling, even when the counselee doesn't seem to resemble a counselee. Even in mundane and annoying encounters, such as one in which the counselee insists on asking you to attend to his wife's depression while ignoring his own, or one in which the counselee faces the agonizing decision about abortion and asks only what the Bible says about it—even in such noncounseling or precounseling encounters, the counselor counsels. That is, the counselor attends and witnesses and reflects feelings. When the counselee points only to his wife not to himself, the counselor witnesses that it is difficult to have to face or listen to oneself or to take responsibility. When the counselee demands answers, the counselor is not defensive or pedagogical about not delivering them but reflects the counselee's fervent wish for such easy deliverance, or perhaps simply the counselee's honest expectation from past experience that delivering answers is what pastors do.

The counselor takes a leap of faith into the graciously alien reality of counseling, and thereby invites the counselee to leap, too. If there are initial anxieties (for either counselee or counselor) or if feelings of trust and safety develop hesitantly, the counselor does not try to conquer the anxiety or hesitation by resorting to usual "relationship-building" techniques, such as five minutes of small talk at the outset or an exchange of jokes. The counselor lives with and witnesses to the anxiety or hesitation (unfettered by a need to build a relationship). It is precisely the gift of counseling that the trust is rooted in such safe embrace of the anxiety, not in the worldly contrivances that would disguise the anxiety and manufacture a trust.

If conversation is initially stymied, this is not an emergency that requires the abandonment of counseling to maneuver things back on track. ("Surely you must have some feelings about that which you can tell me." "We can't make much progress if you can't remember more about that." "I know you would like my opinion about that, but counseling goes better when we hear from you.") The stymie is just part of the process, not an emergency, and can be recognized as such as part of the counselor's steady nonchalant regard. ("This kind of conversation takes some getting used to." "Things want to come out, and they don't want to come out, at the same time.") Such initiation into counseling is part of counseling, not preliminary to it.

Some communities define the role of pastor as an authority called to intervene and to deliver remedy—a role that is incompatible with the understanding of pastoral counseling expressed here. Some individuals, of any community, have a desperate and understandable need to have their pastor speak directly for God and to pronounce. When such a subculture confronts the subculture of counseling, there is no need to debate or resolve these issues, to establish who is "right" before proceeding to counseling. That is irrelevant. What is important is that these needs, hungers, expectations, these ties to roots and custom all exist and are present and are in conflict, here and now. We can live with that, the counselor and counselee discover—and maybe also with other conflict and stress.

NAMING THE PROBLEM: THE COVER STORY

A crucial transition dilemma arises from the counselee's inexperience and discomfort in telling his or her story clearly and candidly. The counselee cannot name the problem. This deserves extended discussion, more or less as a prototype of all the transitional dilemmas.

Alice approaches you to talk about missing cleanup Saturday. Her intense and insistent manner suggests a larger and more intimate distress than that. But she talks about the cleanup episode. Murray flags you down with some urgency as though he has something nagging him—and it turns out eventually that he does. But he starts out talking about Sam, as people often start out talking about others. Sometimes it's the traditional, "I have this friend who . . ." Sometimes it's, "I wish you would speak to my husband about . . ." Somebody else asks you what the Bible says about forgiveness. A father is worried about the reputation of a religious cult his teenage daughter is interested in.

When the counselee explains, at the outset, why counseling is requested, this "presenting problem" is usually an incomplete and a disguised explanation. It has to be. A big part of the distress that occasions the counseling is the confusion and perplexity. Distress seems to be coming from nowhere, or from everywhere. If the counselee had the insight and the courage to know accurately and fully what the full problem was, he or she would not likely be looking for counseling. It is the goal of counseling, not a prerequisite for counseling, to move from a partial and discrepant self-understanding to a more whole and honest self-understanding. Tersely put, it is the goal of counseling to discover the problem and not necessarily to move on to the "solution."

This "presenting problem," this initial self-understanding, is sometimes called the "cover story." The cover story is not a false story. It is a comfortable version of the true story. Like the cover of a book, it hints at what is inside, even while it protects the contents. Like the cover of a package, the cover story discloses the general contours of what is being covered, but obscures details. The cover story is a here-and-now version, or a "for now" version, of the self story. The cover story reveals and disguises. The cover story is a metaphor, communicating what cannot be expressed more directly.

You don't deal with the cover story by turning your back on it, but by looking carefully at it. The cover story is the self-understanding the counselee is comfortable with presenting—for now. If that self-understanding deepens, it will be the result of the safety the counselee comes to feel from having this cover story acceptingly witnessed to.

Even when the opening story seems open and candid, it still can be called a cover story, since it turns out to have depths and details only implied at the outset. Grief is a common example. The grieving person usually presents profound and raw feelings of loss and pain. We can safely surmise and may discover that there are more painful feelings present, such as angers, longings, guilts, the turmoil of unfinished business and unsettled relationship. But we don't delve or pry. We witness the cover story as is. The grief is a compact package. However much it does or doesn't unwrap and unravel, witnessing to one part is witnessing to the whole. The cover story represents and gives access to the whole.

Pastoral counseling is *not* detective work. Moving towards increased self-understanding does not mean that there is *a* true story that must be discovered or counseling is a failure. Quite the opposite. Counseling does not need to move beyond the cover story in order to be effective. The cover story is more "true" than "false." This is because counseling is not addressed to the situation. Counseling is concerned with the meaning the situation has for the counselee, with the affect it triggers. Meaning and affect transcend any situation; they are more general and pervasive than the boundaries of any situation, any cover story. They hover over the cover story, available, even though they also may become more vivid and intense in deeper stories.

Perhaps the most substantial part of Freud's legacy is his insistence on the wholeness of the human personality. Seemingly diverse components are, in fact, connected: the conscious and the unconscious, adulthood and childhood, the emotional and the intellectual, the past and the present, the mind and the body, the trivial and the portentous. Freud writes as lyrically as Paul to the Corinthians about the many members of the one body. Motifs belonging to one component pervade and belong to all. Motifs are encountered where they are encountered.

Theologically, the fact of Incarnation invests the routine and the ordinary with a presumption of significance. If God meets us where we are and does not require a divesting of the daily, we can meet each other and we can meet ourselves where we are. We need not "come clean" before we can be known.

ALICE AND MURRAY

Alice approaches you with regrets and misgivings about not fitting into her place in the church cleanup project. These regrets, misgivings, and quandaries about her role become more lucid and more vivid as she comes to talk about her father's landscaping project and her father's relationship with her. They would become still more vivid and more poignant when and if she talked about earlier years with her father. But we don't need to delve that deeply, we don't need to discuss her father at all in order for the feelings of regret and misgivings about self and place to be present and to be the material of counseling.

Even if the counselee is tied to the cover story and does not move beyond it very rapidly, the counselor is not tied to the cover story. This is not because the counselor is privy to a better story so much as because the counselor is not tied to *any* story. The counselor's attention floats above the content and listens for the meaning that transcends any particular content. So the counselor witnesses aloud that Alice is upset about not being where she thought she belonged, or maybe just that Alice is upset, but not that Alice is upset over the church cleanup project. So the counseling proceeds about Alice's sense of belonging and not belonging, or her sense of missing out, her pain over disappointments suffered and disappointments rendered. This happens—counseling happens—whether these upsets are situated for now in the church project or in her relationship with her father.

Murray accosts you for a late evening conversation: "I was talking with Sam before the meeting and thought you ought to know what he is going through. Maybe you should talk with him, or maybe find him some volunteer work to do in the church office." It's a rather breathless and intense remark, affect spilling out. (Perhaps this moment is *not* unusual for Murray. Perhaps he frequently scouts needs for pastoral attention or recruits for church jobs; perhaps he has a special guardianlike relationship with Sam; perhaps he is just a busybody. That would affect drastically what you hear in Murray's outburst. But let us suppose not; let us suppose that this is a special moment, a special intensity.) The "story" Murray tells doesn't seem to be enough to warrant his urgency. There must be more story. More of *Murray's* story, that is. Of course there is more to Sam's story, "what he is going through." But what Murray "is going through" is not very evident, only that he is upset.

If that is what you hear, what do you say? There seem to be four choices.

(1) You can take the cover story at face value and talk about Sam. Murray's intensely ambivalent feelings about work are present whether he is talking about Sam or himself, and if it turns out that he does not consciously connect them with himself in your presence, your counseling has still done its work if you have made those feelings clearer and more comfortably available to Murray.

(2) You can recognize it as a cover story and surmise what it may *reveal* about Murray. Perhaps he feels a kind of survivor guilt for outlasting Sam at the office, perhaps he identifies with Sam's plight. Perhaps Murray has urgent needs to feel useful, a good scout, a minister's assistant, God's vicar.

(3) You can take the story as an effort to *conceal*—since that is what cover stories also do—and dismiss it as such. "OK, I'll talk to Sam, but what do *you* really need to talk about?"

(4) If you hear it as the ambivalent, conflicted, multiple-layered remark that it is, both revealing and concealing, you can accept it as such. "You sound pretty worked up. Just from talking to Sam?" Or, "Talking with Sam seems to have triggered a lot of stuff for you." Maybe, "So, you've figured out what Sam needs; if it were only that easy for the rest of us."

The last option, just hearing Murray's remark as it is, seems the most natural and easiest, and spares the counselor from having to muster wit and acumen to probe and ferret out. I think that in the last option, also, Murray will have the best opportunity to see himself, and see himself known and regarded, and will feel most safely enabled to face himself still more clearly and more wholly.

GOOD ENOUGH COUNSELING

Freudian analysis lingers in our culture as one kind of prototype for pastoral counseling, but it lingers as a daunting model. Whatever else one may say about its techniques and theories, Freudian analysis is intimidating because of its demands. It requires a huge investment of time (Freud himself raised the possibility that it may in fact be "interminable."). It requires huge and subtle and well-honed talents of discernment by the therapist. It requires a huge capacity by the therapist to be ascetic, to withhold personal involvement and relationship, to stay discreetly out of sight even. Even if one dismisses Freud as a therapeutic model, these demands hover. Freud expresses for us at least the fantasy of a kind of perpetual suspension, while everything is peeled back and turned over and analyzed, until *the* key problem is identified—*the* peculiar psychological gene, as it were, that is flawed and needs to be repaired.

This fantasy of investing skill and time into finding and resolving the real problem—the fantasy of the perfect or ideal counseling—is not part of the world of pastoral counseling. People are more whole and self-pervasive than that kind of mechanistic model. We don't need to look behind what the counselee is saying to discover what the counselee means. We don't need to wonder whether the counselee would be closer to the "real problem" if he or she were talking about a relationship with parents, rather than with a boss, or maybe a relationship with spouse or God or children. Whichever setting, situation, or relationship is on the table, counseling is talking about the hopes and fears and chagrins and commitments and all the rest of the panoply of the soul. We can witness to whatever we witness and know we are witnessing to the person. We can accept whatever sector of life at whatever depth of account the counselee offers as our access to him or herself. It is good enough counseling—not an apologetic statement but a celebratory one.

When counseling has ended, it may be true that another session might have revealed more and accomplished more. But that would not make it more perfect—maybe more complete, more whole—but not more perfect. For perfect counseling is a Golden Calf, an idol we can get along without.

Counseling as God's Call

Some nagging questions haunt the preceding chapters: Is this *pastoral*? Is this way of dealing with human distress faithful to the call one claims, to be God's minister to God's people? Or is it distraction from that call? Clearly, this model of pastoral counseling deviates from many conventional hallmarks of ministry. It does not attend particularly to religious beliefs, to membership in a religious community, to religious practice, to religious ethics, to religious service, to religious scripture. Insofar as one's ministry is defined by such criteria, the pastoral counseling portrayed in this book seems not to fit. To adopt this approach to counseling is to raise questions about those criteria of call. No wonder the questions nag.

This chapter suggests that there are theological criteria of call and ministry which afford sounder warrant and authority for ministry—and for pastoral counseling—than these conventional hallmarks of ministry, which are largely cultural and not distinctively Christian. That is, these "things" of religion are more or less characteristic of all religions in all cultures—public liturgy, private prayer, credal orthodoxy, moral probity, institutional loyalty, scriptural literacy. They locate a minister and church in the cultural matrix. This is how popular culture recognizes ministry. But, if the prophets are to be heeded, such religious apparatus is not always highly endorsed by God.

We must look deeper to find the reason for being, the soul, of ministry—that which calls a person to be an agent for God's ministry to the world, that which defines and sustains that ministry, that which makes pastoral counseling pastoral. For that we must invoke the powers of Creation, the persistence of God's grace with its uncanny attraction to the outcast and alienated, the rhythms of justification that preserve the demand for justice while transcending it, the mysterious power of Incarnation, the dialectic of a God becoming utterly immanent in order to call us to an utter transcendence, the paradox of God and ministry self-emptying in order to be fulfilled, the eschatological summons to live in the present as though we were already beyond it. In gracious sum, by affirming God's doings, we may take the stress off of our own doings and may trust in our own being.

GOD'S BENIGN SOVEREIGNTY

The pastoral counselor affirms, above all, that this is God's world and that the counselor and counselee are both in God's care. So the counselor is relieved of the need and deprived of the option to intervene and take control of the counselee's life, to take responsibility for resolution and remedy. The counselor may not and need not guarantee a positive outcome. The counselor may not and need not feel guilt for apparent "failure." The counselee's ultimate well-being does not depend on the counselor's performance, for the counselee is in God's care. Nor does the counselor's ultimate well-being depend on his or her performance, for the counselor is in God's care.

Counseling as God's Call

Is the counselor a witness to God's activity, or does the counselor assign God to be witness of his or her own performance? A counselor's eagerness to know, to diagnose, to analyze, to prescribe, to manage, to set agenda, to design, to define goals for the counselee and to accomplish them—all this fervor contradicts the affirmation of God's benign sovereignty, is contradicted by that affirmation, and reproduces the conditions that have brought the counselee to feel the need for counseling. These cannot be the components of faithful counseling. They maim and constrict. They harbor idolatry. They offer cheap and unreliable grace.

The faithful counselor so marvels at God's endlessly resourceful power to create afresh and unimaginably, to surprise, that the counselor deems it a high privilege to witness this creative power up close in the life of another. The faithful counselor so marvels at God's determination to use the debris and casualties of life in amazing re-creation that the counselor is enabled to witness that debris—"as is" and "as though" we have said—unblinking and amazed. "Witnessing" regains for the counselor the traditional evangelical overtone of testifying to what God can do.

Perhaps a pastoral counselor's question of faith comes down to this: Is God's Creation sufficient? Or, does it need more? Does it need correction and supplement? Does the Creation hold within it sufficient resources for the correction of distortion and damage? Dare the pastoral counselor accept the entire Creation "as is," as sufficient? The distress and distortion that bring a counselee to counseling—is this part of a Creation that can embrace and absorb it? Or is it an attack by alien or demonic power against a fragile Creation that needs heroic protection—from the counselor? Is this God's world, or is the world—as early Manichean heresy would have it—the battleground between Godly and demonic powers? Is the counselor called to trust or to battle? Is the counselor a spectator, a witness, to a sovereign God and a sufficient Creation, or is the counselor a gladiator defending a smitten God and an infirm Creation? Which does the counselor trust to be stronger and to prevail: the Creation as endowed by God or the fallenness with which humans have stained the Creation?

Is the counselor of Alice and Murray a companion on their religious pilgrimages to find meaning and mission in this world? Or is the counselor a rescuer who endows them with superhuman magic or who plucks them away, as in a flying saucer, to an extraterrestrial haven?

Physicians constantly face the question of whether to invade with pharmaceuticals and surgery or to let be and protect and nurture. When I am physically ill, I sometimes panic, or my doctor may. My pain and fear and doubt and unknowing make me want a heroic warrior to intervene with out-of-this-world powers. The world "as is" appears to be failing. If my doctor says, "Take two aspirins, rest, and call me in the morning," that seems puny and fumbling, and subjects the doctor to caricature (as does the counselor who says things like "I hear your pain"). It places the healer on the sidelines, not in the fray. Yet such casual response—witnessing from the sidelines—may be precisely the appropriate recognition of bodily resources that do their own healing given a little protected time-out.

Is the Creation sufficient? Apparently God has faced this question and made a choice. In opting for the strategy of Incarnation, God has chosen to rely on the Creation. Humans need not be called out of their own lives to be saved.

God has relied on life "as is" as the arena for saving. Pastoral counseling has warrant and model for practicing a similar act of "incarnation," a participation in the life of the counselee as it is, trusting in its created integrity to find its way. The pastoral counselor testifies to the grounds for blessing the counselee's life, "So be it."

SELF-DISCOVERY BY SELF-SURRENDER

To the Christian, finding the self by losing the self is a fundamental principle of moral and spiritual development. It is also more than that. In the New Testament, it is also a characterization of God and of God's redemptive strategy. As such, it becomes a model, if not a mandate, for exercising a ministry in the name of this God.

As always, the Christian view challenges the conventional, popular, common sense view. In all human cultures, a god is, by definition, the supreme wielder of power, the controller of human destiny, often arbitrary. The God who, from the peak of Mount Sinai, issues detailed regulations for the management of life is no exception. Such a God is a tempting model for ministry and counseling, managing others' lives—for their own welfare, of course—from aloofness and with detailed regulation. But the New Testament portrays a very different kind of God, a God encountered not on a throne or mountain peak or tempest, not aloof and unseen. The New Testament portrays a God choosing to be encountered in the exile of an obscure manger, in the person of itinerant teacher, sometimes reviled and often misunderstood, in the words of homely parables and in the humble rhythms of daily life, and on a mean cross. The New Testament portrays a God who renounced being God for the sake of being God, a God who could heal and save and make whole and holy, one who "emptied himself . . . humbled himself and became obedient to the point of death—even death on a cross" (Philippians 2:7f).

Such a revelation calls a ministry that renounces the conventional trappings of ministry—a ministry of reigns and reins—for the sake of a ministry of healing. Ministry is the art of making space for others to grow, this ministry in the name of One who saves by surrendering Himself. Ministry makes the commitment that it is others who are to loom large. Ministry is the constant sharpening and shaping of questions, more than the giving of answers. Ministry is the giving up of authority and status and acclaim in ways that help others to discover their own authority and status and claims. Ministry is in moving beyond the assumption of roles—recognized, defined patterns and guidelines, agendas for popularity and checklists for accomplishment—into raw encounters with people at their thresholds of growth, where there is chaos before there is form. Ministry is in renouncing self and in renouncing all the structures that define ministry, because the structures ultimately falsify and impede ministry. Ministry is in going, radically, to the people as they are, rather than insisting that the people come to the minister.

Such a revelation calls a counselor to renounce the status, expertise, authority, and responsibility that may, conventionally, seem to make counseling *pastoral*—to renounce this for the sake of making counseling *pastoral*. It is a starkly radical surrender, not an exchange of one identity for another, but a surrender of identity altogether, a sacrifice as all-out as God's. One must be prepared to have others not recognize one's role or effect; no plaudits or appreciative testimonials (except for the occasional tribute which, perhaps like some of the Palm Sunday cheering, is excruciating because it is so inappropriate). One must be prepared to get along without being able to tote up, at the end of an hour, a day, a career, any checklist of accomplishments (except for the inevitable moments when one succumbs, perhaps like the Palm Sunday rider, to accepting conventional popular criteria). This is what happens when a pastoral counselor is not a pastoral counselor, a minister is not a minister, God is not a god. Like God choosing to live, at least for a term, not apart and for Self but in the life of an Other, and for the sake of others, the pastoral counselor chooses to live, at least for the term of pastoral counseling, not apart and for self but in the life of an other, for the sake of that other.

ESCHATOLOGICAL HOPE
(AS IF: THE SUBLIME SUBJUNCTIVE)

Pastoral counseling as portrayed here is sometimes judged "unrealistic," as presupposing that the counselee has sufficient motivation, skill, freedom, and personal support to confront the self and to change. The beginning counselee, it is argued, is treated as though he or she had already accomplished successful counseling and had achieved insight, maturity, strength, faith, hope, and love. The beginning counselee is regarded as though he or she were freed from the matrix of distorted relationships and distorted fears, angers, and loves that caused the griefs that brought the person to counseling. The person who manifestly feels alienated from the life intended for him or her, and alienated from the kingdom in which he or she is intended to live—is regarded as though already living that life in the kingdom.

To such accusations, pastoral counseling can proudly plead guilty. To the stubborn reality of regarding people "as is," pastoral counseling blends the stubborn unreality of regarding people "as if."

The so-called "nonviolence" commitment of Mohandas Gandhi and the Reverend Martin Luther King, Jr.—like the so-called "nondirectiveness" of pastoral counseling—is in fact a radically positive affirmation far transcending a label of "non"-anything. They share the totally "unrealistic" commitment that their adversaries are already converted, already committed to the values of justice and equality; that commitment just needs to be identified and liberated from the fears and angers that smother it. Gandhi and King—and pastoral counseling—regard others as if they had already transcended the plights of the present, as if they already lived in the promised future. The strategy of pastoral counseling, like that of Gandhi and King, is to dissolve some of that tangled knot of fears and angers that obscure the promise and strangle the future.

It is not just raw, unmitigated hope that pastoral counseling displays, for that is deadly. Hope by itself becomes a norm that judges and measures nonfulfillment. The pastors most afflicted by hope become the first to burn out. Perhaps it is the counselors most afflicted by hope who become most impatient with pastoral counseling and resort to psychological management techniques. Hope by itself loses its bout with reality. Gandhi's and King's martyrdoms become just two wasted deaths. Hope without love becomes badgering insistence. Hope without faith becomes anxious, driven. The pastoral counselor does not just lodge in the present, discerning its starkness and wishing for something better. Any counselor can do that. The pastoral counselor actually believes that the new age symbolized by God's Incarnation has already begun, and that we can reliably offer to each other, in our faith, lodging in the kingdom.

It is tempting to find pragmatic cover for such exposed faith, to argue that believing makes it so or that regarding makes it so. We could cite the classroom research in which, for example, when teachers are told that their students have high (or low) IQs, their students come to *have* higher (or lower) IQs. When a counselee is treated like someone, he or she comes to feel like someone. This is probably true; regarding "as if" comes true. But pragmatic reasons for faith sabotage faith. The counselor's "as if" belief in the promises the counselee can live by derives from faith in the efficacy and reliability of God's promise, not from faith in the efficacy of her or his own belief.

PASTORAL COUNSELOR
AS PRIEST AND PROPHET

It is common to define Pastor (and therefore Pastoral Counseling) by contrasting it with the roles of Prophet and Priest. The contrasts are easily carried to extremes and sometimes to debate. The typologies vary: Pastor, Prophet, and Priest are said, respectively, to be turned inward, outward, and upward. They foster, respectively, self-centeredness, other-centeredness, and God-centeredness. They convey, respectively, grace, responsibility, and holiness. Traditionally, Prophet and Priest are accorded distinct Godly commission and access. Each is heard to speak for God, and each is heard to speak to God, as Pastor is not.

But these tidy distinctions are too casual, too peripheral, and too polemical. The more deeply one reflects on these modes of ministry, the more they resemble each other in essential characteristics. Even if each refracts ministry in its own way, it is the same ministry. We do better to try to comprehend that ministry, rather than just the refractions. In particular, here, we can better understand "pastoral," better understand what is essential and fundamental about "pastoral," by understanding "prophetic" and "priestly."

The Priestliness of Pastoral Counseling

From the very beginning of human history, we have felt an insistent Other relentlessly impacting our lives, or threatening to, and we have needed to set someone apart to be a mediator with It. Beyond human compass, alien to it, the Other is experienced as having superhuman power, as being enveloped in mystery, as potentially hostile, as demanding. (In contemporary terms, this is how we regard illness, economic cycles, extraterrestrial beings, and much of our own emotional life.) The priest has been set apart to deal with the Other. The priest is not necessarily expected to control or subdue or even to understand the power and mystery and demands; such countering of the Other is impossible and unnecessary (or requires a magician). The priest has been set apart to live with it, to communicate with it, even to befriend it. In Christian priesthood, as in other priesthood, this intent is paramount.

In primitive consciousness, early in history and early in childhood, the priest is sometimes understood as negotiating, as bargaining. The priest is the broker of this-for-that transactions between the people and the Other. But in more mature consciousness, the priest aspires to no more, and no less, than communication, mutual awareness, a kind of mutual incorporation. The priest's effects are on consciousness, self-consciousness. The priest raises consciousness. People do not necessarily *behave* differently as a result of the priest's mediation; rather, they *see* themselves differently, for having been brought into relationship with the Other. Likewise, it may be presumed, the Other does not necessarily change, but does see Itself differently for seeing Itself in relationship with the people.

It is illuminating and not distorting to make this description of priesthood a description of pastoral counseling. Pastoral counseling aspires to just such awareness and self-consciousness as a result of communication with, and befriending of, powers that loom out of reach, out of ken, clouded with mystery and awakening dread. Pastoral counseling doesn't change these powers or the person encountering them, but does foster a readiness to live with them as they are. Pastoral counseling, too, has its primitive stages, recurrent moments in which there is temptation to think one can bargain and negotiate ("I will do this or that in exchange for a promise that I can receive that or this."). But this conditional mode of living is exactly what pastoral counseling wants to surpass in order to attain that kind of unconditional nonchalance—live and let live—to which the priest aspires.

To enable the mediating role between a people's life and the Other that prevails beyond that life, the priest is stationed beyond the everyday life of the people. The priest is set apart, perhaps behind a wall and screen (as in Orthodox worship or Roman Catholic confessional), perhaps uniquely garbed, perhaps handling objects the people are forbidden to touch, perhaps speaking language unknown to the people, perhaps renouncing some defining portion of daily life, such as sexuality or family living. For the duration of priesthood, the priest is not "one of us."

For essentially identical reasons, the pastoral counselor finds ways to be set apart, not to be involved in the kind of matrix of relationship that "normally" characterizes the counselee's life and to be remote enough to provide the counselee surcease and freshness, an undefensiveness that affords openness and communication.

Attempts to democratize the priesthood—as in "the priesthood of all believers"—make demands that believers can seldom meet or else change the meaning of priesthood. It is not always the laity who urge democratization. Priests are often uncomfortable with being set apart, and laity are often uncomfortable without a set-apart mediator. (Correspondingly, in pastoral counseling, it may often be the counselor who is uncomfortable with being set apart, out of the action, and who wants to be chatty friends with the counselee.)

On the other hand, although the priest is set apart, the materials of the priest's practice are almost always the most mundane and ordinary extracts of daily life, things like bread, wine, candles, sheep, and words. It is a delicate tightrope act to keep communication open and plausible between people's ordinary lives and the holy Other. These objects and the priest's use of them must convincingly maintain solidarity with the ordinary even as they must also convincingly transcend the ordinary and reach the Holy.

Pastoral counseling similarly conducts its transactions with the vocabulary and stuff of everyday life, yet does so in a way that transcends and illuminates the ordinary. The counselor finds ways to speak of bosses and spouses and fears and angers in ways that are both immediately recognizable ("Yes, that is me you are reflecting") and freshly illuminating by representing a wholly transcending perspective. ("I see myself differently." Maybe even, "I see myself whole," or, "I see myself as I was meant to be.") The delicate art of staying just a half step ahead of the counselee is not unlike the priestly art of keeping sacraments rooted in the ordinary but also magnificently transcending the ordinary.

Prophetic Pastoral Counseling

To understand the biblical concept of a prophet, we can rely on Walter Brueggemann's *The Prophetic Imagination* (Fortress Press, 1978). In his succinct portrayal of the prophet's role, we find remarkable congruences with that of the pastoral counselor.

To be sure, both the prophets and Brueggemann presuppose the constituency of the community and *its* growth in self-awareness, whereas pastoral counseling generally presupposes the constituency of an individual or family. But this distinction need not make any difference to the principles of ministry being invoked. I think there is nothing in principle that the prophets and Brueggemann want to say about ministry to a community that cannot be said about ministry to individuals; conversely, the pastoral counseling portrayed here is, in principle, fully appropriate to ministry to a community.

Brueggemann writes:

> *The task of prophetic ministry is to nurture, nourish, and evoke a consciousness and perception alternative to the consciousness and perception of the dominant culture around us.* (p. 13)
>
> The alternative consciousness to be nurtured, on the one hand, serves to *criticize* in dismantling the dominant consciousness. . . . On the other hand, that alternative consciousness to be nurtured serves to *energize* persons and communities by its promise of another time and situation. . . . (p. 13)
>
> [I]f the church is to be faithful it must be formed and ordered from the *inside* of its experience and confession. . . . (p. 15, emphasis added)

> [R]eal criticism begins in the capacity to grieve be-
> cause that is the most visceral announcement that
> things are not right. . . . As long as the empire can keep
> the pretense alive that things are all right, there will
> be no real grieving and no serious criticism. (pp. 20f)

The prophet is not the expert the public expects, not
the teller of the future, not a prescriber for the future. The
prophet is not motivated primarily by any particular social
issue, is not an advocate for any one cause, does not have
an agenda of social policy to impose. The prophet is not
out primarily to change people's behavior, but instead
wants to change people's awareness and self-perception
in a way that will change their approach to *any* issue they
may face. The diagram near the end of chapter 1 in this
book applies equally to prophet, pastoral counselor, and
priest; all three are working at the left end and trusting the
person and community to work on the right end. The
prophet, like the pastoral counselor, aims at a conversion,
a rebirth, a refreshened identity. But the new identity is
not new; rather, it is a return to what is truest. The prophet,
like the pastoral counselor, relies on the resources already
within the tradition of the community.

What the prophet aspires to is a liberation from the
"consciousness and perception of the dominant culture
around us." And that is precisely what the pastoral counselor aspires to, a freedom from, and disregard for, those
constricting judgments of the self with which the "dominant culture around us" has captured and throttled us. But
Brueggemann does not say "liberation." That would seem
too passive, something that happens *for* you or *to* you, en-
acted by someone else. Brueggemann says to become *critical* (about the dominant culture around us) and *energized*
(by the prospect of new life ahead). Such proactive agency,

the responsible living out of self, not just the release of self, would be the hopes of the pastoral counselor too.

The prophet, Brueggemann suggests, has little traffic with "systematic" theology, the overarching, balanced, comprehensive, and abstract view of matters, "under the aspect of eternity." (p. 24) The prophet practices a partisan theology, always for the moment, always for the concrete community, satisfied to see only a piece of it all and to speak out of that at the risk of contradicting the rest of it. Prophet and pastoral counselor both, apparently, take with an ultimate seriousness the immediate experience confronting them and take it "as is."

The prophet, according to Brueggemann, is not a heavy-handed scold. The prophet does not command a position ahead or above or aloof from the people, does not appraise from a neutral distance, does not stand at the goal line in the spotlight of justice and righteousness and beckon people to come. The prophet "nurtures and nourishes and evokes" the strengths the people possess unawares.

The prophet stands with the people in their plight and knows that something is wrong because of the visceral grief welling up within the prophet's own terror or pain, a grief that will not be denied, much as the rulers of the world want to suppress it. Pastoral counseling can be energized by the reminder that grief, our staple, is such a subversive power that it cracks open dominating empires and creates radical newness.

IS PASTORAL COUNSELING IMPOTENT IN THE FACE OF REAL TERRORS?

To invoke the heritage of the prophet, however, is to bring us face to face with the gnawing misgiving that pastoral counseling may miss the point. The most fateful problems are imposed on people by social forces and by natural calamities for which pastoral counseling, as known here, has no leverage. Concern with individual feelings and distress may be a massive cover story obscuring the actual crises of life. So we end the book as we began it, with another pass at the question, Why pastoral counseling?

In the face of the apocalyptic facts of life—poverty, cancer, injustice, abuse, and on and on—the reality of pastoral counseling may seem timid, irrelevant, and impotent, an abandonment of the real issues of life, an opiate. In the face of the huge diversities of life—individual diversity and cultural diversity—pastoral counseling may seem to impose a rigid formula, fitting some people and some situations very well but misfitting most. In the face of the urgency and complexity of God's plan and God's call, pastoral counseling may seem a shallow skimming or counterfeit of grand concepts like grace and incarnation. In the face of the richness of ministry as called by God and by the church, pastoral counseling may seem a suffocatingly narrow restriction of the role of pastor, zealously forsaking most of the religious resources and responsibilities with which the ministry is endowed.

These are important and common objections to pastoral counseling as portrayed in this book. They need to be taken seriously. But what does it mean to take such misgivings seriously? That's the question of the preceding chapter. Does taking them seriously mean that they have to be countered and vanquished before counseling can begin? Or does taking them seriously mean that they are to be profoundly listened to, in the mood of counseling? Must dissent and dilemma be dealt with as prerequisite to counseling, or is the atmosphere of counseling prerequisite to dealing with the dissent and dilemma?

Counseling as God's Call

Pastoral counseling of course cannot change the facts of poverty or other injustice, abuse, oppression, alcoholism, psychosis, cancer, atheism, or depression. But pastoral counseling is profoundly committed and effective in energizing people to address such facts, changing what they can and coping creatively as they must.

"Of what use is grief counseling," one might ask, "when it can't change the fact of death or any other loss?" It only "adjusts" people to the death. To ask that question is to answer it. But to answer that question is to focus more clearly on the next question: What about things that can be and should be changed, not adjusted to? Pastoral counseling aspires to enable people to take their place as responsible citizens of God's world, as agents of God's redemptive hope for that world. But it does not assign them to this mission or instruct them in how to carry it out. It is more effective because it is indirect. Pastoral counseling exercises the discipline to be disinterested in the dismaying facts of life just because it takes them so seriously, seriously enough to mobilize people's best resources for contending with them. Pastoral counseling exercises the discipline to disregard the facts a counselee recounts because it so profoundly regards what transcends these facts: namely, the meaning that they convey to the counselee. The postures of hope or despair, attack or submission, trust or fear, isolation or participation—these make the difference in how the person lives life and contends with whatever impedes and disrupts life. To reclaim commitment and clarity, to beget faith, hope, and love, to find life affirmed—this is the conversion of soul that sometimes happens in pastoral counseling.